MW01115574

ASTROLOGY AND HOMOSEXUALITY

yes!

Yes! Inc.
1035 31st St. NW
Washington DC
20007-4482
(202) 338-7874
(202) 338-2727

ASTROLOGY
AND
HOMOSEXUALITY

Wim van Dam

Translated from the Dutch

SAMUEL WEISER, INC.
York Beach, Maine

First published in Dutch in 1983 by
Uitgeverij Schors, Amsterdam, Holland
Original title: *Astrology & Homofilie*
© 1983 Uitgeverij Schors

First published in English in 1985 by
Samuel Weiser, Inc.
Box 612
York Beach, Maine 03910

ISBN 0-87728-628-0
Library of Congress Catalog Card Number: 84-52178

Translated by Transcript, Ltd., Clevedon, England
Typeset in 11 point Bembo by
Positive Type, Millerton, NY
Printed in the United States of America

CONTENTS

LIST OF CHARTS

PUBLISHER'S NOTE

This is a book that is sure to be controversial, and indeed has already evoked varying reactions from many who have read it prior to publication. Homosexuality is a controversial subject for a variety of reasons. We would like to stress that this is a research work, intended to be used by serious students of astrology who wish to become involved in research that may eventually lead to the ability to determine the difference between homosexuality and heterosexuality in the birth chart. This book was not written to council homosexuals, nor was it written to "cure" homosexuals, nor was it written to condemn.

Very little is available in the astrological literature on the subject of homosexuality. In his attempt to restructure an approach to researching astrological indicators in the birth chart, the author has gone back to the only significant study on the subject: Karl Heimsoth's *Homosexuality in the Horoscope*, first published in German in 1928, and available in English since 1978, published by the American Federation of Astrologers, Tempe, Arizona. We wish to thank the American Federation of Astrologers for graciously giving us permission to use the data from Heimsoth. The reader should understand that the Heimsoth material presented here may appear in a slightly altered translation than the English version. The material contained herein was translated from German into Dutch, and from Dutch into English. We found that the meaning was clear, and decided to use the author's presentation. The charts from Heimsoth's work have been reproduced from the original Dutch edition.

The charts used in this book do not include birth data so that the identity of the people involved will be protected. The author has informed us that the charts were calculated according to birth records and have not been rectified in any way.

INTRODUCTION

The subject of homosexuality is much discussed in the astrological world, and many strongly held opinions are being bandied about concerning it. It is all the more surprising, therefore, that not much has been published on the subject. The lack of published material could be caused by the fact that the various assumptions and conclusions of traditional astrology have not yielded practical results when applied to actual charts.

For this reason, it seems useful to devote a special study to this topic. We are not starting this study by using one or two vague rules previously presented in most textbooks—usually the cause of homosexual behavior is ascribed mainly to Uranus and Neptune. The technique applied here (the Navamsa, or ninth harmonic chart) will be fully explained in Chapter 4 and is illustrated by a number of examples. Many astrologers are still relatively unfamiliar with this technique and it is hoped that the example charts provided will persuade them that navamsa positions form the real key to the horoscope in many respects, and not only when it comes to homosexuality.

Regard for the privacy of clients is, of course, a delicate problem. The charts of several well-known European public personalities whose sexual proclivities are general knowledge (Gerard Reve, Wim Sonneveld) are used with names. As far as other example charts are concerned, the place, time, and date of birth are withheld to protect their identities. However, the sidereal time and the latitude are supplied so that astrologers who use some other house system than the one employed here (Placidus) will have the chance to experiment for themselves. A little juggling with the data will reveal the date, but not the exact G.M.T., and therefore not the longitude. The latter has to be determined from the place of the Moon, and this is always corrected for so-called parallax.

Although this book contains some interesting and promising conclusions about homosexuality in both men and women, as well as discussing differences between the sexes, the last word has still to be said on the matter. It is the author's hope that the techniques used and the material offered will prove a stimulus and a help to others who wish to research further.

My special thanks are due to Mrs. van Opstal-Koelen, who has provided me with a great deal of valuable material. Without her assistance this book would not have appeared in its present form. I must also express my gratitude to the many other astrologers who so willingly supplied me with data from their own collections, and to my publisher who gave me the idea for the book. The responsibility for the conclusions drawn is entirely mine.

1. WHAT IS A HOROSCOPE?

Not every reader will be perfectly familiar with the materials used by an astrologer in his work. This first chapter has been written to provide a brief description of what is meant by a horoscope.

The night sky is filled with an expanse of *fixed* stars which, as their name suggests, appear to form an unchanging pattern with one another. Although the sky itself seems to slowly revolve, and these stars revolve with it, the star pattern stays the same. We simply see the same pattern from different points of view. In contrast to the fixed stars, there are other heavenly bodies which are continually changing their position, both in respect to the fixed stars and to themselves: they wander in their path across the face of the sky. These are the Sun, the Moon and the planets (planet means *wanderer*). The Sun, Moon and planets are represented by the symbols shown in Table 1 on page 2.

The Sun, Moon and the planets (Mercury through Saturn) are traditional elements which have been used in astrology for thousands of years. Uranus, Neptune and Pluto (and now Chiron) have been discovered comparatively recently. The Dragon's Head (Moon's ascending or North node) is not a planet but one point of intersection of the orbits of the Sun and the Moon. Directly opposite it is the corresponding Dragon's Tail (or Moon's descending node which is also called the South node).

Table 1. Planetary Symbols

Planet	Symbol	Planet	Symbol
Sun	☉	Saturn	♄
Moon	☽	Chiron	⚷
Mercury	☿	Uranus	♅
Venus	♀	Neptune	♆
Mars	♂	Pluto	♇
Jupiter	♃	Dragon's Head	☊

Astrological significance is traditionally ascribed to the nodes, although they are not rated as highly as the other heavenly bodies.

Every year the Sun appears to follow the same track through the fixed stars. The circle it describes is known as the ecliptic or, more familiarly, as the zodiac. The Moon, the planets, and the lunar nodes also move through the zodiac, but each at its own pace. As seen from Earth, the Moon moves through the ecliptic in 28 days. Mercury and Venus take about a year, Mars nearly 2 years, Jupiter 12, and Saturn 29 years. Chiron takes 56 years, Uranus 84, and Neptune 165, while Pluto completes the course in 250 years. The Moon's nodes take 19.

The planets are divided into those which are favorable (benefics) and those which are unfavorable (malefics). The benefics are Venus, Jupiter and, as far as we know, Chiron. The malefics are Mars, Saturn, Uranus and Pluto. The Sun and Moon are neither benefic nor malefic, and Mercury takes its color from the planet with which it is most closely connected. Nothing certain is known about Neptune on this point.

The astrological meanings of the planets are easily understood as "keywords." In addition to the basic keywords or meanings shown in Table 2, the planets have other, more concrete significations. Thus the Moon also symbolizes a

Table 2. Keywords for the Planets

Planet	Keywords
Sun	Power, vitality, self-consciousness
Moon	Instinct, emotional contact
Mercury	Mental contact, communication
Venus	Harmony, union
Mars	Energy, aggression
Jupiter	Expansion, rising force, warmth
Saturn	Limitation, contraction, downward force, coldness
Chiron	Balance, completion
Uranus	Revolution, originality, the unexpected
Neptune	Vagueness, the indefinable, art, deception
Pluto	Regeneration, transformation, the underground
Dragon's Head	Personal and family contacts

person's nation or mother; Venus, the spouse; the Sun for the spouse *and* for the children; Saturn for the authorities and for the father; Mars for sport and war, etc. The particular meaning of a planet in a given chart which comes most to the fore depends on the position held by this planet in the different parts of the horoscope.

The zodiac starts at the first point of Aries. Each spring, the Sun crosses the celestial equator in its journey through the zodiac; at that moment it stands directly over our own equator. The point in the zodiacal band where it then stands (a point which very slowly shifts against the fixed stars) is, by definition, the commencement of the zodiac and, as already indicated, is known as the first point of Aries, or 0° Aries. The position of the

Table 3. Keywords for the Signs

Sign	Symbol	Keywords
Aries	*Ram*	Active, spontaneous
Taurus	*Bull*	Possessive, slow, materialistic
Gemini	*Twins*	Quick, changeable, talkative
Cancer	*Crab*	Home-loving, protective, maternal
Leo	*Lion*	Self-aware, creative
Virgo	*Virgin*	Critical, attending to details
Libra	*Scales*	Harmonious, peace-loving
Scorpio	*Scorpion*	Fanatical, secretive, penetrating
Sagittarius	*Archer*	Purposeful, striving
Capricorn	*Sea-goat*	Cautious, ambitious, authoritative
Aquarius	*Water-bearer*	Unorthodox, fickle, unpredictable
Pisces	*Fishes*	Vague, impossible to pin down, philanthropic, impressionable

Sun, Moon and planets in the zodiac, known as planetary *longitude*, is their distance from this starting point measured in degrees. However, astrologers do not talk of a planet having a longitude of 45 or 172 degrees. The zodiac is divided into twelve equal sections of thirty degrees each: called Aries, Taurus, Gemini, and so on. A longitude of 45 degrees is called 15° Taurus; 172 degrees becomes 22° Virgo. As soon as a measurement exceeds thirty degrees, we commence from 0 degrees again but in the next sign. The movement of the Sun and the Moon through the zodiac is always in a forward direction from the first to the second sign, but in a counterclockwise direction. When viewed from Earth, the planets can appear to move backwards through the zodiac at times. This phenomenon is known as *retrograde motion.* However, for the most part planets display a direct motion, although not a constant speed. The lunar nodes always move retrograde, with a speed of some nine minutes of arc per day.

Keywords for the signs are listed in Table 3. The odd signs (Aries, Gemini, etc.) are male and the even signs (Taurus, Cancer, etc.) are female. Wherever we are on earth, half of the zodiac is always above the horizon and half beneath it. Planets in the upper half are in the day half of the zodiac, and planets below the horizon are in the night half.

Owing to the diurnal rotation of the earth on its axis, the zodiac appears to revolve around any given place of observation on Earth in about a day, and the planets, of course, turn with it. Therefore all the planets, the Sun and Moon included, revolve once a day round every fixed observation place on Earth. While they are being carried along by the zodiac in this way, the planets are also moving through it much more slowly. Like the zodiac itself, this daily trip round the earth is also divided into twelve sections: six above the horizon and six below it. These are the so-called *houses* of the horoscope, and each planet moves through each of the twelve houses every day[1]—quite unlike its very laggardly journey through the twelve signs.

In contrast to the signs of the zodiac illustrated in Figure 1 on page 6, the houses are nowadays[2] left unnamed, but are generally known as the first house, the second house, etc. However, they have their own special meanings, as shown in Figure 2 on page 7.

The significance of the houses is more concrete than that of the signs. The houses represent facets of life; the signs provide more of a psychological description. However, a comparison of the signs and houses does reveal a relationship between the two equal-numbered sets. The second house has to do with money and possessions, and the second sign, Taurus, is heavily involved with the ownership of material things; the seventh house represents

---

[1]It would be truer, perhaps, to say that the houses rotate past the planets. *Tr.*
[2]I have added "nowadays" because the Greeks and Romans named them. *Tr.*

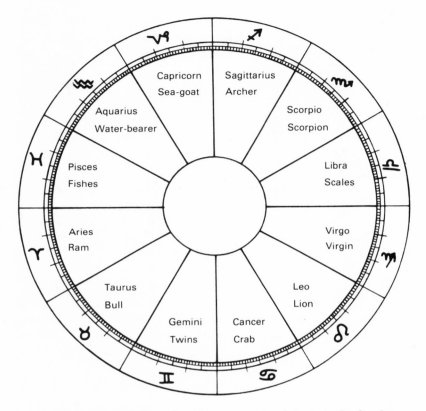

Figure 1. The signs of the zodiac. As you can see, Aries is in the first house position and the signs proceed counterclockwise.

the partner (both in love and in business), while the seventh sign, Libra, focuses on harmony and collaboration. In practice the significance of the signs and houses run hand in hand. The individual whose chart has many planets in the fourth house will develop Cancerian characteristics, even if there are no planets in Cancer in the natal horoscope. However, the student will do well to look on the signs as revealing character traits and the houses as showing the concrete circumstances of life.

The change-over points between the houses are called *cusps*. Each house has its own cusp. In its daily journey through

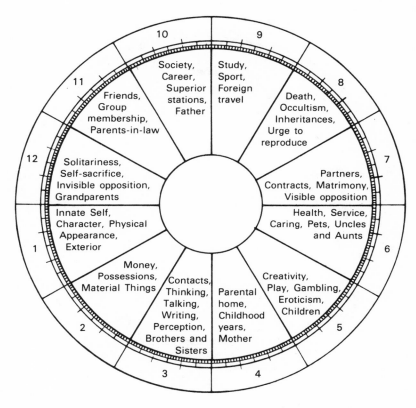

Figure 2. An illustration of the natural houses with a brief description of house meanings.

the houses, a planet moves in a clockwise direction, and at the end of every house it crosses the cusp of that house, the most sensitive point of the house. Therefore a planet is always to be found in one of the twelve signs of the zodiac and simultaneously in one of the twelve houses. This already gives for each planet 12 × 12 = 144 basic positions. The place of a planet in the signs is called its *zodiacal* position, and its place in the houses is the *mundane* position.

It is important to note that the houses do not necessarily contain thirty degrees of the zodiac (as the signs do), but seem to

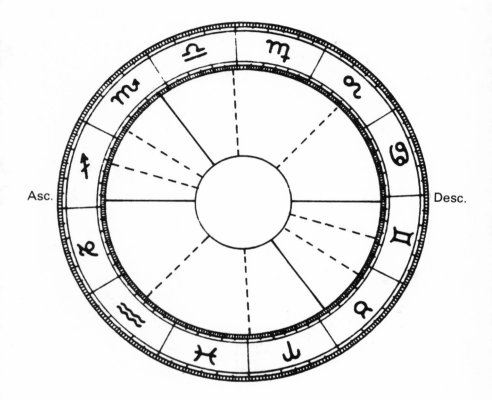

Figure 3. An example of house division. Geographical latitude 51°30′; sidereal time 14.00 hours (2PM). The cusps of the angular houses (1, 4, 7, 10) are indicated by solid lines. Note that Sagittarius, Taurus, Gemini, and Scorpio each contain two cusps, but there are no cusps in Capricorn, Pisces, Cancer and Virgo. The last four signs are intercepted.

be distributed rather capriciously over the zodiac. And so it can happen that there are two house cusps ruled by one sign, while another sign may have no cusps at all. (See Figure 3.) A planet in a sign that has no house cusp is known as an *intercepted* planet. According to tradition this weakens the influence of the planet.

So a chart is a diagram representing the position of the Sun, Moon, planets, and lunar nodes (both in the zodiac and in the houses) at the moment of birth, as seen from the place of birth.

There is no unanimity of opinion in the astrological community over the precise division of a chart into houses. Formerly, the great majority of astrologers employed the system of diurnal and nocturnal semi-arcs devised by Maginus (1555-1617) and further developed by Placidus (1603-1668), for whom the house system is named. The Placidus system will be used in this book, for I find that it gives by far the best results.

An astrological chart is fairly easy to calculate. The positions of the planets in the zodiac can be looked up in *ephemerides*, which are annual astronomical tables that provide the longitudes of the Sun, Moon and planets for each day of specific years. The houses are determined from *tables of houses*. These give the cusp positions for every degree of terrestrial latitude and are not dependent on the year of birth, so that a table of houses is valid for any birth year.

The positions of the planets in sign and house can always be calculated objectively or, to put it another way, their calculation always leads to one astronomically correct result. However, additional material is used by astrologers which allows more freedom of interpretation—with all the attendant advantages and disadvantages of that.

There are recognized relationships between the planets and the signs. Each planet has a sign or signs where it fits in well and can express its nature to best advantage, and each planet has other signs where it is considered ill-placed. When a planet has a particularly close affinity with a certain sign we say that it is the *ruler* of that sign. When, on the other hand, it is at cross-purposes with a sign, we say that it is in its *detriment* there. The Sun and Moon rule one sign each; the planets traditionally rule two each, as illustrated in Figure 4 on page 10. The lunar nodes (Dragon's Head and Dragon's Tail) have no rulership.

A planet is in detriment in the sign that is six signs away from the sign it rules. Thus the Sun is in its detriment in Aquarius, Mars is in its detriment in Libra, and so on. In the remaining signs, where its position is neither good nor bad, the

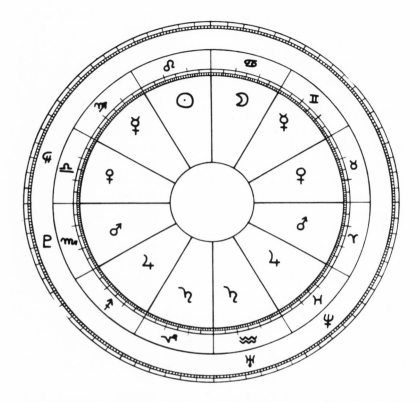

Figure 4. The signs shown with their natural rulers. Cancer and Leo have been placed at the top of the chart to make it easier to see how the remaining classical planets taken in turn have a double rulership on either side of the Sun and Moon. The more recently discovered planets are placed in the outer circle, adjacent to their alloted signs.

planet is said to be *peregrine*.[3] The reason why the Sun and Moon only rule one sign, whereas, according to tradition, the planets rule two signs each, is that the planets are bisexual and can rule two signs of different sex. The Sun is symbolically male and is

[3]Technically, a planet is only peregrine if it has no essential dignities (of which rulership is merely one) and is not in mutual reception with some other planets (the two planets concerned being mutually posited in each other's essential dignities). *Tr.*

ineligible to be lord of a female sign, while the Moon, as purely female, is ineligible to be lady of a male sign.[4]

A planet that is not posited in its own sign is *ruled* by the lord or lady of the sign it's in. So the Sun governs any planets which happen to stand in Leo, Jupiter rules planets in Sagittarius and so with the rest. The significance of a planet for good or ill is determined partly by the position of its ruler (or *dispositor*). For example, planets in the sign of Cancer will be better off when the Moon is well placed than when the Moon is in Capricorn (in her detriment).

A planet also rules the *house* cusp when that cusp is in that planet's sign. The native whose ascendant (the cusp of the first house) is in Taurus will have Venus as ruler of the ascendant. The ruler of the ascendant is always a significant point in the chart, even though it may not be as important by definition as some astrologers would have us believe. (The student would do well to regard the Sun, Moon, Mercury, and the ruler of the ascendant as the most characteristic planets or points in the horoscope. Which of these is the most decisive factor in a given chart can be determined only by experience.) As we have seen then, a planet can rule a sign as well as other planets *and* houses. Great emphasis is laid on the ruler of a sign that also rules many planets and an important house cusp.

It is now time to consider another part of traditional astrology, namely the *aspects*. As measured along the zodiac, each planet is situated a certain number of degrees from some other planet. This distance is always measured along the shortest route and varies from nought to 180 degrees. Some of these distances are important: it is considered very constructive when two planets are separated by 120 degrees. In contrast, a distance of ninety degrees is full of tension. Constructive or tense angles are called *aspects*, and each aspect is, in principle, either *hard* or *easy*. When two planets occupy the same place, that is to say at a distance of nought degrees, they are said to be *in conjunction*. In

---

[4]Male and female here have no relationship to people or sex. This is actually a definition of an idea. Male and female represent concepts in this sense. *Pub.*

Table 4. Astrological Aspects

Aspect	Degrees Apart	Effect	Type
Conjunction	0°	Neutral	Major
Semisextile	30°	Easy	Minor
Semisquare	45°	Hard	Minor
Sextile	60°	Easy	Major
Quintile	72°	Easy	Minor
Square	90°	Hard	Major
Trecile	108°	Easy	Minor
Trine	120°	Easy	Major
Sesquisquare	135°	Hard	Minor
Biquintile	144°	Easy	Minor
Inconjunct	150°	Hard	Minor
Opposition	180°	Hard	Major

itself, a conjunction is neither good nor bad: everything depends on the nature of the planets involved, as well as on the signs in which they are found. A conjunction of the Sun and Jupiter in Leo will usually have a constructive effect (the Sun in its own sign in conjunction with a benefic), but a conjunction of the Moon and Saturn in Capricorn is not so fortunate (the Moon in its detriment and in conjunction with a malefic). The most difficult aspects are those with malefics in their detriment; when, for instance, Saturn is in Cancer, even a trine may work out badly in the end. The aspects are shown in Table 4. Even the aspects between planets and angular cusps have some import; the conjunction is usually the only aspect noticed between planets and the house cusps. A planet that makes many hard aspects is known as an *afflicted* planet.

Of course, the distance between two planets is scarcely ever exactly 90 or 120 degrees; there is always a certain amount of leeway which we call the *orb*. For the major aspects, most astrologers allow an orb of 5 through 8 degrees, for the minor aspects 1 through 3 degrees. The more exact the aspect, the stronger will be its effect. An exact minor aspect has a more noticeable effect than a wide major aspect. We should mention, too, that most astrologers do not use all the aspects listed in Table 4; in particular the quintile, the trecile (or sesquiquintile) and the biquintile are—unjustly—little used, mainly because they are hard to recognize. The multiples of thirty degrees are easier to see and therefore are the most commonly used. All astrologers agree on the value of the major aspects, but hold varying opinions about the orbs involved.

At the beginning of the present century many astrologers were inclined to treat a trine between two planets as invariably favorable and a square as invariably unfavorable. Nowadays, however, the old insight that the outcome of the aspect is also determined by the nature and placement of the planets involved, is slowly coming back into favor. Thus a square between Mercury in Virgo and Jupiter in Sagittarius (two planets well placed, one of them a benefic) will not do much harm. A sextile between Saturn in Leo and Mars in Libra (two malefics in their detriment) promises "heavy weather." Therefore to evaluate an aspect correctly requires careful judgment.

Finally, some astrologers still make use of the fixed stars. When a cusp or a planet is in conjunction with a bright fixed star, it is subject to the influence of the latter. Several books deal with this subject; the best is probably Vivian Robson's *The Fixed Stars and Constellations in Astrology*[5]. The fixed stars sometimes give brilliant results, and at other times appear to do nothing. Therefore, in natal astrology (astrology dealing with horoscopes of individuals) the fixed stars have to be handled with care and

---

[5]Published in England by the Aquarian Press, Wellingborough, and in the United States by Samuel Weiser, Inc., York Beach, Maine. *Tr.*

are apparently not sure-fire. In mundane astrology, which has to do with current affairs, these stars play a leading part.

The planets, signs, houses, and aspects have been presented to give the student a brief review of traditional astrology. We can now resume the theme of this book, which the question of whether or not it is possible to identify homosexual tendencies from the natal horoscope.

2. CONSIDERATIONS REGARDING HOMOSEXUALITY AND HEIMSOTH'S WORK

Surprisingly little is presented in astrological literature about indications of homosexuality in the horoscope. The sexual inclinations of an individual are usually well-defined in later life, but their connection with horoscopic patterns is seldom mentioned in our textbooks. The following material is an overview of previously published theories.

Ptolemy, the father of Western astrology, says in his *Tetrabiblos*, Book IV, Chapter 5, that if a man has Mars in aspect to Venus and Jupiter, and if the latter two planets *precede* the Sun, the individual will confine his sexual interest to men. He also says that the presence of Mars and Venus in masculine (odd) signs in aspect to one another inclines women to be lesbians.

Jeromo de Cardano (1501-1576), the reputed discoverer of a mathematical rule which he allegedly filched from Tartaglia, wrote that the presence of Mars and Venus in feminine (even) signs in the *western half* of the chart (houses 4, 5, 6, 7, 8 and 9) causes men to be homosexual. The placement of the same planets in masculine signs (odd signs) in the *eastern half* of the chart (the remaining houses) supposedly makes women uninterested in male lovers.

In more modern times, Charles Carter (one of the leading astrologers of the twentieth century) has written in his *Encyclopaedia of Psychological Astrology* that the real key to homosexual behavior is to be found in the more recently discovered planets Uranus and Neptune. These are particularly liable to cause homosexual behavior, he thinks, when involved in an opposition in Taurus/Scorpio, out of houses five and seven, and also involved with other suitable planets. He has named as especially critical zones, 25° Leo and/or Aquarius, and 8° Aries and/or Libra. Of the two planets, he considers Uranus the more important indicator of homosexual behavior.

By and large, this is also the opinion of most modern writers. Usually this point of view is reduced to the dictum that a badly aspected Uranus in the horoscope is liable to make the native homosexual. Hard aspects between Uranus and Venus, and also the conjunction of these two planets, have the same significance to most astrologers. This position is also adopted by Dutch astrologer Mellie Uyldert in her *Astrology II* (p. 202),[6] where she writes that homosexuals often have Venus-Uranus aspects in their horoscopes, but that these aspects do not always represent homosexuality.

Possibly it is true that conflicts or conjunctions between Venus and Uranus more often occur in the horoscopes of homosexuals than they do in charts of heterosexuals, but that does not mean that they stand for the predisposing causes of homosexuality. The present writer has a conjunction of Venus and Uranus, but is not aware of any homosexual inclinations. What is more, many of my acquaintances have strong links between Venus and Uranus in their charts, but homosexuals are few and far between among them.

The significance of this constellation is something rather different: Venus reveals love relationship, and Uranus stands for caprice, unexpectedness, splitting and tearing. It is hardly surprising that this planet was discovered in 1781, on the eve of the French Revolution, which put an end to the "Ancient Régime" and ushered in the "New Age." It is easy to see that conflicts between the two planets can have an unfavorable effect on the love life, as can the presence of a badly aspected Uranus in

---

[6]As far as we know, this work has not been translated into English. *Pub.*

the seventh house (the house of relationships, marriage and collaboration). With this planetary position an easy-going relationship spanning several decades is highly unlikely.

Homosexual relationships seem to be more liable to break down than do heterosexual ones. There is no need to consider here whether this is due to the nature of the relationship itself or is due to social factors (the presence of children or an official marriage contract may act as restraining factors or provide social pressures for heterosexuals). More significant is that the love life (as a whole) for the average homosexual is more explosive than that of the average heterosexual. This is what may be shown by the presence of Venus-Uranus conflicts in the horoscopes of homosexuals. Venus/Uranus conflicts in the horoscopes of heterosexuals would show explosiveness as well.

A somewhat similar explanation has been proposed for another phenomenon that we sometimes observe in the horoscopes of homosexuals—namely the presence of several planets in the twelfth house. One might think it would be fairly easy to confirm this theory but we are again faced with the reality that groups of heterosexuals also have planets in the twelfth. The twelfth house is the house of solitariness and seclusion, and the presence of important planets in this house points to a retiring life, whether voluntarily so or not. Traditionally, we also find this kind of astrological placement quite frequently in the charts of monks, hermits, celibate priests, prisoners serving long sentences, bed-ridden patients, etc. Obviously planets in the twelfth house have nothing to do with homosexuality as such.

Owing to the disapproving attitude adopted by society towards homosexuality—certainly not so very many years ago—many homosexuals saw no alternative but to have a secret love life, away from prying eyes. Also the discovery, often in youth, that one was "different" must have led to reclusiveness; especially in view of the influence of the church, which nearly always condemned this disposition. There has been an increasing social tolerance of homosexuality in recent years, and the influence of religion has weakened, so that it is entirely possible that twelfth house placements in the horoscopes of homosexuals are currently less prominent. So although we have here a possible connection between planetary configurations and homosexuality, the connection is not hard and fast because, in fact, it is with something that is not an essential part of homosexuality but attached to incidental social pressures. As for the alleged influence of Uranus in connection with homosexuality, a well-known Dutch astrologer once informed me that he had formed the opinion (from extensive statistical research) that Uranus afflictions were not especially prominent. Instead he felt it was Neptune which seemed to be a prime indicator of homosexuality. Carter, of course, had already sensed the importance of Neptune.

For a subject which has always aroused such interest, surprisingly little has been published on this subject, while other topics such as blindness, divorce, musicality, aggressiveness, murderousness, diabetes and, in recent years, fatal road accidents (Kuypers) and anorexia nervosa (Hamaker-Zondag) have often been successfully investigated from an astrological point of view. Certainly, the interest is there, and most astrologers have a few horoscopes of homosexuals in their files in which a perfunctory search has been made for likely signs but apparently with few clear results.

The only judicious study, as far as I know, which has ever been devoted to this subject was *Charakter-Konstellation*, published in Munich in 1928, and written by psychiatrist Karl Heimsoth. In 1978 an English translation of this work was published by the American Federation of Astrologers under the title *Homosexuality in the Horoscope*. We provide a short review of the book, not only because it is the only significant study containing both a wealth of material and a coherent theory, but also because it provides good insight into a new rather outdated way of thinking which was very popular in the twenties.

Heimsoth endeavored to forge a link between orthodox Freudian theory and astrology. According to the Freudian school of psychoanalysis, it was natural for every boy to form a love-tie with his mother in his earliest years, making him hate his father (the famous Oedipus complex). By a normal development, these feelings of love would later be transferred to other women who would then command his devotion. However, certain traumatic experiences in early life were considered to produce disturbances in this development (neuroses), thus hindering a subsequent normal transference. The outcome was a permanent, if unconscious, attachment to the mother which might be so intense that it prevented the individual from enjoying a deep and satisfying relationship with any other woman after reaching adulthood. Therefore the male feels compelled to consort with members of his own sex for the satisfaction of sexual needs. This would appear to hold no threat for the one really important relationship, namely the relationship with the mother. The same reasoning was applied to female homosexuality, but in regard to the father. According to the Freudian group, the person concerned should engage in a long series of sessions with a psychiatrist, in which word associations, dreams and slips of the tongue would all be used by the latter to bring to light the trauma which caused the neurosis in the first place. As soon as this trauma has been restored to conscious memory, the patient will presumably be "cured" of the disorder and will become heterosexual. Few people take such a simplistic view today. But in the 1920's this kind of psychoanalysis was very popular in progressive circles.

What Heimsoth tried to do in his book, *Homosexuality in the Horoscope*, was to find a connection between the neuroses which he thought must form the basis of the homosexual lifestyle and the weak points in the horoscope. In his opinion, every retrograde planet in a horoscope pointed to a neurosis. The same is true, he said, of each planet in an intercepted sign, *i.e.* in a sign in which there is no house cusp (see Chapter 1).

By this token, there is scarcely a horoscope that does not indicate at least one neurosis, for at least one planet is nearly always retrograde or intercepted. With this idea as his starting point, he deals with thirty or so horoscopes and elaborates on the astrological significance of the neuroses he sees contained in them. It is noteworthy, however, that not all the example horoscopes provided belong to definite homosexuals. In some cases, Heimsoth merely comments that there were evidences of

innate neurotic behavior and then, without more ado, adds that
the reason lay in a latent homosexuality. He jumps to the same
conclusion when an individual has a difficult love life (for
instance the Prince of Wales, who later became King Edward
VIII and abdicated the crown in order to marry the American
divorcee, Mrs. Simpson) or when a person's chart indicates little
sexual desire.[7] To a Freudian this would be clear evidence of an
underlying neurosis, and thus of latent homosexuality. An
instance of this type of repression is proposed in the person of a
young man who felt an excessive sympathy for the sad lot of
prostitutes and was constantly trying to "rescue" them from
their profession. Heimsoth says, "To the psychoanalyst such a
'bordello complex' is considered a strong indication of a latent
homosexual component." In this chart, too (his Figure 8 shown as
Chart 16 on page 60), as might be expected, it is not hard to find
many signs of neurosis. (He also says that the use of narcotics is
hard evidence for homosexual inclinations!)

   The arguments employed by Heimsoth to stamp his
patients as homosexuals are sometimes so far-fetched they are
comical. Of one case, the Scandinavian F.H.,[8] who suffered from
potency problems, he remarked that his fiancee "belongs to the
boyish type that is so much in fashion today." If this type of girl
was so much in fashion, the patient would obviously have had
difficulty in finding one of another type!

   Another example is Case Number 6 (our Chart 15 on page
59), where Heimsoth described the patient as a very thin,
somewhat feminine young man who in regard to sex considered
himself completely normal; he was strongly opposed to the idea
that there is a certain degree of latent homosexuality present in
everybody. Heimsoth felt that direct astrological evidence of
homosexuality was indirectly supported by events that came to
light during analysis. A.G. (Chart 15) was on a walking tour with
a friend, and due to shortage of accomodations they shared a bed

---

[7]See Heimsoth: *Homosexuality in the Horoscope*, horoscopes 7, 19, 22 and 29, for further
discussion of this idea.
[8]See *Homosexuality in the Horoscope*, K.G. Heimsoth, American Federation of Astrologers,
1978, Fig. 3, pp 37-43.

one night. Although the following night they slept in separate beds, his friend woke up bathed in perspiration and, jumping onto a table in the room, declared that he had just suffered from a nightmare in which he was being chased by snakes. The friend went back to his own bed but was so frightened that he moved over as much as possible to *one* side of the bed. This friend had no knowledge of dream symbolism and was later embarrassed when he realized the snakes from which he had been running away where five to six inches long. Heimsoth felt that the dream must have been occasioned by something which had happened the previous night. Although this is a pretty anecdote, certainly, it is definitely not evidence of any homosexuality in the patient called Case 6. Whether anything took place the night a bed was shared is not clear, but, in view of the friend's behavior, it would be more appropriate to analyze the friend for suppressed homosexuality, leaving Case 6 out of this.

The main conclusions drawn by Heimsoth concerning homosexuality and astrology are as follows: Homosexual behavior is the result of a neurosis. A predisposition to neuroses is strongest in what Kretschmer called the leptosome or asthenic type: a long, thin body, small chest and shoulders, long limbs with weak muscles and an oval face. Heimsoth associates this with Aquarian and Geminian types, and to a lesser degree with Scorpios. He then goes on to discuss the "tall, aristocratic figure" so often ascribed to noblemen (for example to the "English gentlemen"). This, he thinks, is strikingly accompanied by homosexual inclinations and, indeed, in his Chapter Nine, he lays a charge of homosexuality against almost all the European dynasties. Of the planets, Uranus is the villain. Its position in the fifth house, intercepted, retrograde or badly aspected (preferably by Venus) is a sure indication of homosexuality. And if the native is unaware of any such impulses, this is considered even more powerful evidence that he possesses them—unconsciously! and suppressed!

Heimsoth has little to tell us about female homosexuality. In the two pages (Chapter Seven) devoted to this subject, he asserts that female homosexuality is entirely different from the male variety, that it is something with which we shall eventually catch up, and that "active" lesbians may be expected to have an overemphasis of masculine signs or strongly placed masculine planets in their charts. The more passive type would, he conjectures, be characterized by Neptune in the seventh house. Uranus plays here a more minor role than in male homosexuality. Given the nature of Neptune (vagueness), Heimsoth concludes that the female homosexual is much more chaotic than her male counterpart, and also claims that lesbians "are really frigid for the most part." I leave this for the ladies to decide. Unfortunately Heimsoth supplies no sample horoscope for lesbians.

Apart from its psychoanalytical approach, in which the author was no more than a child of his particular age, Heimsoth's book is a valuable contribution to the study of homosexuality and astrology. For the first time in history, a separate study was made of the subject. There is no need to blame Heimsoth for the fact that his conclusions were colored by the era in which he wrote. That is unavoidable. In this area of study we are outside the confines of the exact sciences. My own work is based on the principle that as few assumptions should be made as possible, except for the assumption that homosexuality is going to be represented in the horoscope somehow or other. We shall suspend judgment on whether or not homosexuality is a disease, a neurosis or an evil perversion, as even Carter considered it to be (he listed it under "I" for immorality). The basic premise in this book is that sexual preference, whether or not it is moulded by heredity or environment, is a neutral phenomenon, which is not always easy to determine (asexuality, bisexuality). Perhaps in fifty years' time this material will also seem out of date.

3. RESEARCH PROBLEMS

As it happens, astrological research into homosexuality has not progressed much beyond the hypotheses discussed in the previous chapter. It is somewhat painful to have to admit it, but the traditional astrological techniques presented in Chapter 1 seem unable to aid sensible observations in this area in practice. And, sad to say, this is true not only of homosexuality. Astrologers often realize that we find no systematic indications which are particularly noticeable in one group that has a certain characteristic, or in some other group from which that characteristic is absent. For instance, an investigation of the horoscopes of children suffering from mongolism (Down's syndrome) has never led to concrete results. Of course, it is not hard to find something "wrong" in the chart of a given person suffering from this condition and to offer this as "the" indication; but it is frustrating to discover that this same indication is absent from the chart of another person suffering from the same disease. We are therefore compelled to search for alternative indications.

Since every horoscope has its bad points, we can always find them, but what we really need is a clear-cut indication that frequently occurs in mongoloid children's charts—something that happens very infrequently in the charts of normal children. The same concept applies, naturally enough, to any group we wish to define using astrological indicators to ascertain particular characteristics. This situation makes astrologers acutely uncomfortable. Is the horoscope able to provide data in respect to such important things as sexual proclivities and mental capacity?

The dissatisfaction felt on this account has led many astrologers to see that although the traditional techniques described in Chapter 1 form the basis of astrology, they are not sufficient in themselves. There must be something that will draw aside the veil from the horoscope to reveal hidden dimensions, and there have been numerous attempts to discover what this elusive something is. A well-known example is the system of midpoints developed by Alfred Witte at the turn of the century and further elaborated by Reinhold Ebertin. In this system the midpoint is determined between each pair of points in the chart (Sun/Moon, Sun/Mercury, Sun/Venus, Moon/Venus, etc.). If the Sun is 3° Scorpio and the Ascendant is 3° Aquarius, then the Ascendant/Sun midpoint is 18° Sagittarius. A study can be undertaken of the effects of the angles (0, 45, 90, 135 or 180 degrees) made to the midpoints from the usual significant points in the chart. Thus it is thought to be unfavorable when the Sun/Ascendant midpoint forms one of these aspects with Saturn. Some astrologers also take into account the aspects of midpoints to one another. Obviously, such a procedure is going to release from every chart a flood of indications providing the answer to any question one cares to ask. Sad to say, it is almost impossible to distinguish correct information from incorrect in this welter of indications. Even the advocates of the system are regularly heard to sigh, "If only I knew a method of differentiating in advance between important and trivial midpoints!" Naturally, by important is meant those midpoints which provide accurate information.

As a matter of fact, some supporters feel that the apparently strong side of the midpoint system (that it invariably supplies some very telling indications) is actually its weak side (that there are plenty of inapposite indications). They have therefore accepted an essential reduction, looking solely at the conjunctions (and maybe the oppositions) between midpoints and the usual radical positions. They no longer worry about angles of 45, 90 and 135 degrees—thus cutting down the number of contacts by a useful 75%. Satisfactory results have still to be announced, but this approach is certainly more rational than the original method. We are also spared the irritating question of why the moderately important 45 and 135 degree arcs were employed but not the traditionally stronger and more important angles of 120 and 60 degrees.

Another technique that has been proposed in many variants is that of the so-called "mirror points." In this system, the shortest distance from a planet or cusp to a given point is measured, and then the same distance is marked off on the other side of that point. For example, Mercury at 1° Leo has a distance of 24 degrees from the Sun at 25° Leo: these 24 degrees *added* to 25° Leo give a Mercury "reflected by the Sun" position of 19° Virgo. Other systems use 0° Aries or 0° Cancer (antiscion points) for reflection, or perhaps some specially defined point for each planet and cusp. Here again there are plenty of extra points for use in interpretation, though many less than if one used all the midpoints.

A very curious development by some schools of astrology, laboring under a sense of dissatisfaction with existing techniques, is the postulation of new planets unknown to astronomy, for which they even publish tables. The biggest splash in this respect has been made by Alfred Witte's Hamburg School, which employs some eight planets of their own invention (Cupid, Hades, Zeus, Chronos, Apollo, Admetos, Vulcan and Poseidon), in combination with the array of midpoints already described. An enthusiastic protagonist once boasted to me that for every horoscope this gives about 5600 indications! No wonder everything can be explained by the system. No wonder, too, that it is a mass-producer of incorrect conclusions as the astrologer has so many choices of aspects that can be interpreted.

Many similarly hypothetical planets are in use all over the world. In America, the astrologer Charles A. Jayne employs the hypothetical planets Pan, Isis, Hermes, Osiris, Midas, Lion and Moraya; in the Netherlands, the Ram School employs Th.J.J.

Ram's conjectural planets Persephone, Hermes and Demeter, the existence of which are accepted as proved without further argument. At the time of this writing, none of these schools has demonstrated in carefully researched reports that relevant conclusions can be drawn only by using these hypothetical planets. But, in any case, we have reason to question these estimations when we remember that, according to the Witte School, an astrologer must rely chiefly on intuition in selecting the indications to be interpreted. From the Ram School we understand that astrology is primarily a system of "divination," that the horoscope signifies nothing in itself but serves merely to stimulate the paranormal powers of the astrologer. The Ram School theory actually supports something which the opponents of astrology have always contended: astrology is irrational, and when an astrologer can do things beyond the power of others (such as foretelling the future, or supplying striking details about the lives of people whose names are completely unknown) it is done by exercising telepathy or clairvoyance.

Emphasis needs to be laid on the fact that these different schools have all proposed the existence of different planets, and that they display little interest in any others than those thought up by themselves. It is interesting to note that the genuinely existing planet Chiron, discovered at the end of 1977 by the American astronomer Charles Kowal seems to correspond to none of the hypothetical planets. Even Pluto was not located by any astrological school before its discovery. It is true that the Dutch astrologer Thierens, among others, had conjectured around the turn of the century that there was another planet beyond the orbit of Neptune, and had even bestowed on it the name Pluto, but no one had pinpointed its position even approximately.

Our original problem—to determine indicators of homosexuality in a chart—remains unsolved in spite of all the above attempts. All too often we see that in either a positive or negative sense, exceptional people seem to have virtually the same charts. To illustrate this idea, let's look at the charts of two cases of *microcephaly*, a congenital defect in which a child enters the world with literally too little brain in its skull. Both children (natal Charts 1 and 2 on pages 28 and 29) lead a purely vegetable existence: they can take in and digest their food but they do not develop, and there is no question of their having any proper contact with the outside world.

If astrology is to mean anything, it should at least enable us to find a reasonable indication for this defect and preferably one that is the same in both horoscopes, at least in part. The demand that the astrologer should be able to make the precise diagnosis *microcephaly* without further information is not very fair: the condition lies so far outside the ordinary person's world of experience that an astrologer might be hard put to it to identify it without more ado. The horoscope merely supplies the building blocks which the astrologer has to sort out and fit together into a comprehensible whole. However, it is certainly fair to expect that the astrologer should notice a predisposition for a serious contact disturbance or a life lived in isolation in both cases.

Take a look at the planetary positions shown in the outermost ring in Charts 1 and 2. Both birth times were given as exact by the parents. Something can be said at once about Chart 1 as the most striking configuration is a very close conjunction of the Moon and Saturn in Aries, in the eighth house. In medical astrology, the Moon stands for the brain among other things, and Aries represents the head. Saturn stands (in principle) for limitation (or impotence) and in retrospect, we could conclude that this is the chart of someone who is deficient in brains. However this solution has several disadvantages:

• The indication is rather impersonal. If we assume that the Moon/Saturn conjunction is the only significant indication, we have to accept that everyone born on this day during the close conjunction of these two heavenly bodies (duration: at least forty minutes) came into the world with microcephaly. Every time Saturn passes through Aries (two-and-a-half years in every twenty-eight) this conjunction occurs once again.

• There are no precise aspects between the conjunction and the cusps in the chart, which would make this conjunction personal.

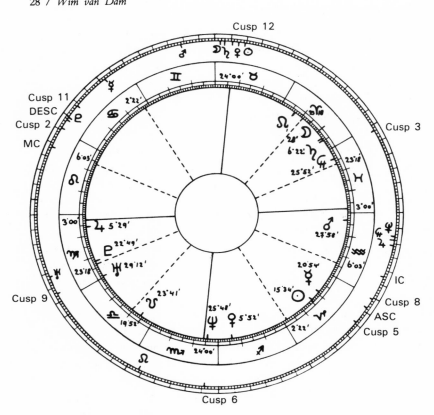

Chart 1. A case of Microcephaly (I).

If the conjunction had been exactly placed on the cusp of the third house (representing the thought processes) it would have been very applicable. Also a position on cusp six (representing the state of health and physical defects) might be an indication. But unfortunately, matters are not so simple in practice.

• The role of the houses is unclear. Since the brain is definitely involved in this condition, and since the brain is usually assigned to the third house in astrology, we might have expected to see this conjunction in the third house rather than in the eighth, standing as the latter does for the dead and for hidden or occult

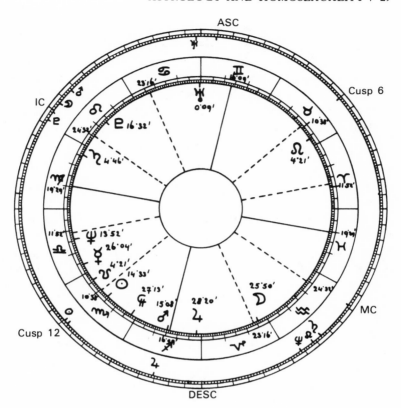

Chart 2. A case of Microcephaly (II).

matters. Of course, we can say that the native is "mentally dead" or that the cerebral functions (Moon and Saturn in Aries) are concealed from us, but that is not a serious solution. If only the Moon and Saturn were ruler of the third house, or made a close square with the lord of the third house, we might be satisfied, but that is not the case. The ruler of the third house is Venus (the classical lady of Libra) or Chiron (its modern ruler), but of these two possibilities only Venus forms an aspect with the two culprits—and this is a trine, and therefore favorable. Those who share the opinion that Chiron is the real ruler of Libra will see with gratification that this planet, as ruler of the third house, is opposed by Uranus, lord of the sixth (representing health problems and bodily weaknesses). There is thus a disturbance (Uranus) of balance (Chiron) in the bodily region (Uranus as ruler of the sixth house), affecting the brain (Chiron as ruler of the third house). However, what we have here is an aspect between two very slowly moving planets, and neither of them is within an orb of one degree in aspect with an appropriate cusp; hence this is not really an individual indication.

• Finally—and here is the strongest argument—if the conjunction of the Moon and Saturn (and perhaps the Chiron/Uranus opposition) is the actual cause of the defect in question, why do we not find a similar indication in the other chart? The same objection applies to any of the indications you may think you have found in one of these two horoscopes. At first glance, the horoscopes have little in common. Can astrologers find any solution to this kind of problem?

4. THE CASE FOR THE NAVAMSA HOROSCOPE

Our last chapter ended with a question which, as it happens, was not intended to be rhetorical; because, yes, a technique does exist that can reveal a striking and singular resemblance between these two superficially so dissimilar horoscopes. This technique avoids all the previously mentioned objections. We refer to the so-called navamsa horoscope.[9] For those who do not know the technique, it is a refinement of a division of the zodiac by which every sign is subdivided into nine signs according to a fixed rule. Great value has always been attached to these derived signs (known as navamsa signs) in Hindu astrology which, we should be careful to note, uses the Eastern (sidereal) zodiac, not the Western (tropical) zodiac. The English astrologer John Addey (1920-1982) discovered that what is involved here is the ninth harmonic (or overtone) and that the traditional navamsa signs can be calculated in a very simple way. Take the absolute length of a point as reckoned from 0° Aries (the beginning of the zodiac) in degrees and minutes, and multiply this value by nine. Subtract 360 from the result, if necessary, as often as is required to make it smaller than 360, and

---

[9]This technique (the navamsa chart) has been discussed in my book *Rectification of the Natal Horoscope*. Chapter 8 provides examples indicating the astonishing results obtainable using this technique. Publisher's note: To our knowledge, this work is not yet translated into English. It was published in Dutch by Schors Uitgerverij, Amsterdam, Holland.

turn this in the usual manner into signs, degrees, and minutes. For example: say the Sun is 2° 30' Gemini; this point is actually 62.5 degrees from 0° Aries. Multiply by nine and we obtain 562.5 degrees which, less 360, is 22° 30' Libra. The Appendix on page 91 provides a table which will enable you to locate the navamsa position corresponding to each point in the zodiac without difficulty.

By so doing you will obtain from every horoscope a second or derivative horoscope, simply by working out the navamsa position for each planet and cusp. It is not very feasible to draw in another horoscope from the derived points, as the reader will discover if the attempt is made, for all the cusps look higgledy-piggledy. The best thing to do, therefore, is to place all the navamsa positions in a ring around the radical chart, in the same way that progressed planetary positions are set out in predictive astrology.

The application of these navamsa positions is very straightforward. Navamsa *signs* are used to find significant shades of meaning for the most important points in the chart (Sun, Moon, Ascendant, ruler of the Ascendant). In Western astrology, notice is chiefly taken of the decanates, for the use of which various systems have been devised, but they have never been adopted very enthusiastically—probably because the results are not particularly convincing. The results are much clearer when you use the navamsa scheme.

The use of the navamsa signs in a supplementary way is traditional in Hindu astrology. So important is this division that no Hindu astrologer will judge a horoscope without having studied the ancillary navamsa horoscope. John Addey's finding, that the navamsa horoscope can be erected not only in signs but in exact degrees and minutes, has led the writer to a notable discovery.

> *When a position in the navamsa horoscope coincides with a position in the radical horoscope or with another navamsa position, this counts for as much as a very distinct ordinary conjunction! The applicable orb is from three to five degrees.*

This is a bold suggestion. The discovery was made by accident but several months passed before the writer could bring himself to make it known, first in a small circle and a little later at the Autumn Congress in Oldenzaal.[10] The theory is an unorthodox one, but it is in fact based on a traditional idea. In the ensuing years it became clear to many astrologers that the technique yielded astonishingly good results. Astrologers who spend time experimenting with navamsa positions will notice that the astrological instrumentarium has become many times more powerful—that many cases in their practice are no longer baffling.

What makes the technique of navamsa conjunctions so attractive is that the number of contacts between horoscopes positions produced by it is quite small (to have more than five in one chart would be exceptional—compare that with the 5600 contacts per chart of the Hamburg school!); so it is certainly no astrological rifle-booth with a prize always guaranteed. On the other hand, the conjunctions which are present will nearly always permit an apt and convincing reading.

Now let us take another look at the two sample horoscopes discussed in the previous chapter. (See Charts 1 and 2 on pages 28 and 29.) The navamsa positions of the Sun, Moon, planets, nodes, and cusps are given in the outer circle surrounding the radical chart. What immediately strikes us in Chart 1 is the accumulation of navamsa positions so dominantly at the top of the chart, where we see the navamsa positions for the Sun, Moon, Venus and the twelfth house cusp in close proximity to the radical MC. Bearing in mind the meaning of the basic astrological concepts (see Chapter 1), it will not take us long to make a few apt interpretations: Cusp 12 (isolation, separation) conjunct M.C. (career in society): the native lives out his life in isolation; conjunct Saturn: due to some limitation or short-coming; conjunct Venus (classical lady of the third house): in the thought processes or the brain.

---

[10]The Oldenzaal Conferences are held once a year in the fall, usually around October/November. For further information, write Stichting Arcturus, P.O. Box 563, 7500 AN ENSCHEDE, The Netherlands. *Pub.*

The above interpretation is further emphasized due to the fact that Venus is also lady (or ruler) of the tenth house. Not only does navamsa cusp twelve stand in conjunction with the radical MC, *but also navamsa MC is in conjunction with the radical cusp twelve!* What is more, the role of Sun and Moon, the two most important natal positions, is not far to seek. Together they symbolize the classical lifegiving force *par excellence.* The Moon is a symbol for the child-bearing and child-caring mother; the Sun is the symbol for the procreating father. The father as teacher and governor is represented more by Saturn. The Sun and Moon together stand for the fullness of life, and here both together are impaired by the conjunction with Saturn and cusp 12. Furthermore, the Sun is lord (or ruler) of the twelfth house, strengthening the significance of that house and its cusp even more.

We previously noted the opposition of Chiron (as lord of the third house) to Uranus represents a disturbed equilibrium in the mental functions, due to some physical defect (Uranus being lord of the sixth house). Although this aspect is very much to the point, it is less applicable to individuals as individuals because the two planets are slow-moving and an opposition between them will remain in force for a long time. However, it is unusually germane that the axis of the navamsa third and ninth houses (the lower and higher minds) should fall exactly over this opposition! In itself the conjunction of cusp nine and the benefic Chiron would most probably be favorable, and could indicate an aptitude for studies, but the good effect is well and truly spoilt by the opposition from Uranus.

Clearly the technique of navamsa conjunctions uncovers the real significance of the first horoscope. Can the same be said of Chart 2, which has to do with an almost identical case? Here, on the cusp of the twelfth house, we have a somewhat smaller grouping consisting of navamsa Moon, Pluto and IC. Here, too, we see that the MC/IC axis (social and domestic life) is directly linked with axis six-twelve (physical defects, isolation). Pluto, a malefic, is lord of the third house (thinking processes, brain).

The navamsa Sun, lord of the twelfth house, stands *with* navamsa cusp twelve on radix cusp three, and the classical lord of the third house, Mars, is in navamsa conjunction with Pluto, the modern lord of the third house; both planets are malefic so their conjunction is unfavorable, the more so as the radical Sun (the lord of twelve) makes a square with them from the sign of Scorpio which they both rule. It was postulated previously that, with navamsa positions, aspects other than the conjunction do not apply; but when a navamsa position is in conjunction with a radical planet, it is affected by all the aspects made by that radical planet. This is nothing else but what is known in astrology as the translation of light.[11] Therefore, we can assume that navamsa Mars is also in square with the Sun in Scorpio.

At first sight, Charts 1 and 2 have little in common, and no close connection with what we know of the natives. On closer inspection, however, they share an unusual "force field," in which the MC/IC axis, the six/twelve axis, Sun, Moon, lord of the third house, lord of the twelfth, cusp of the twelfth house, and a malefic planet all operate on one another. Similar indications, though perhaps not so severe, may also be found in the charts of mongoloid children (children suffering from Down's syndrome).

Chart 2 is slightly less negative than Chart 1. The third house indications are certainly no more positive than those in the first chart, but the mutual interaction of the MC/IC axis with the twelfth house is less stringent. In Chart 1 we are faced with a double MC/cusp twelve navamsa conjunction. In Chart 2 the navamsa conjunction with cusp twelve involves not the MC (social life) but the IC (domestic life), while interestingly enough navamsa Jupiter (a benefic) is in conjunction with radical cusp four, (the IC) in its own sign, which further strengthens the influence of radical Jupiter in the fourth house, also in its own sign. Now why should there be this *positive* emphasis on the fourth house?

---

[11]With all due deference to the author, it is probably right to point out that this is not what is traditionally meant by the "translation of light." Thus in Sibly's *Illustration of Astrology*, 1784, p. 280, we read, "Translation is when a planet separates from the body or aspect of one planet, and immediately applies to the conjunction or aspect of another. And the planet translating is always lighter, except in retrogradation, than the planets from or to whom translation is made." And so Dr Simmonite. *Tr.*

As it happens, there is a striking difference between the domestic lives of the two children. Chart 1 is being nursed in an institution, whereas Chart 2 has already spent its first decades at home being devotedly cared for by its mother (the mother and solicitous care are typical fourth house concepts). Therefore there is a positive (Jupiter) link (Descendant) with the mother (fourth house). So what lessons can we draw from these examples?

• Navamsa positions can offer the key to a true understanding of the horoscope;

• Navamsa positions with a malefic on cusps six and/or twelve are extremely unfavorable, or debilitating to say the least;

• Navamsa positions of cusps are also informative, not only if they are angular houses (Ascendant, MC, Descendant, IC), but also if they are succedent or cadent; see cusps three and twelve (cadent) in these examples;

• In Chapter 1 we saw how, in the astrological world, great differences of opinion exist regarding the correct way of calculating intermediate cusps. The continuous success obtained by the employment of Placidus cusps in the navamsa horoscope is a powerful argument in favor of the correctness of this mode of calculation. Appeal can also be made to other analytical techniques and to systems of progression (in predictive astrology), but there is no time to speak of them in the present book.

• A horoscope has to be accurately cast for the purposes of exactness in individual analysis, and this requires precise knowledge of the time of birth. An error on one degree in a cusp, which may itself have been calculated quite accurately for a time of birth correct within four minutes, will introduce an uncertainty of some nine degrees into the navamsa chart. Seeing that the orb used for a navamsa conjunction is no more than five degrees, interesting indications will be completely lost here. Worse still, there is a chance that incorrect interesting indications will be found which in reality do not exist. If the exact time of birth is not available (and a deviation of two minutes is already too much) or if you are not in a position to calculate the cusps precisely, you will do better to restrict yourself to the navamsa positions for Sun, Moon, nodes and planets. Slight differences in time do not play such an important part here, and the positions of these factors is easy to work out with the help of a good ephemeris.

• Although the technique of navamsa conjunctions originated in Hindu astrology, where use is generally made of the sidereal zodiac, it gives unexpected evidence of the validity of the Western, tropical zodiac. So what are the facts of the matter? If a horoscope is cast in accordance with the sidereal zodiac, which amounts to displacing all positions in the horoscope by approximately 26 degrees, and if the positions of the navamsa longitudes are then worked out from the positions so obtained, it will be discovered not only that other navamsa signs and degrees have been obtained but that the conjunctions are completely different too. In other words: what gives a navamsa conjunction in the Western zodiac, will fail to do so in the Eastern zodiac! But since the combination of navamsas in the Western zodiac provides such clear-cut results, we are compelled to conclude that the oriental technique reinforces the occidental theory.

Armed with this knowledge, we shall now attempt to determine the signs of homosexuality in the horoscope, and the following chapters will give an account of our findings.

5. MALE HOMOSEXUALITY

At the beginning of my study of using the navamsa technique to determine male homosexuality, I assumed that the traditional astrological factors would be present. Venus and Uranus should be noticeably linked in homosexual charts. The link might not be just the ordinary conjunction or inharmonious aspect—but it should be easy to find. I was looking for aspects such as the navamsa Venus conjunct radical Uranus and vice versa. The Venus/Uranus tie was so strongly rooted in my mind that the most that I could consider in addition was that maybe Chiron, or the lunar nodes, might also enter into the picture.

It was very surprising, not to say disappointing, to ascertain after some dozens of horoscopes had been cast and examined that the anticipated pattern failed to emerge. Navamsa conjunctions between Venus and Uranus occur no more often than ordinary aspects do, and certainly no more often than might be expected from a collection of horoscopes made at random.

In retrospect, this result seemed to be quite logical. Even navamsa conjunctions between Venus and Uranus have little that is individual about them. If we were to consider a conjunction of this sort as a decisive factor, we should have to accept that even with a small orb, and a quickly moving Venus, the conjunction would be in effect for at least twenty-four hours. We should then be compelled to conclude that for a period of twenty-four hours,

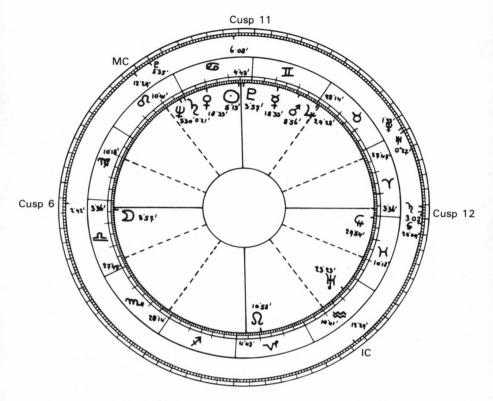

Chart 3. Male Horoscope Number 1. N. lat. 52°05', ST 6h20m34s.

every so often, all male births would bring homosexuals into the world. There might still have been a way to use this aspect if it in turn also made a strong aspect with certain house cusps in the charts of homosexuals, but there was definitely no sign of this.

Hence the decision was made to look for other indications. However, these would have to be suitable to a large group of people. A navamsa conjunction between Jupiter and the Ascendant should, if it were encountered with striking frequency, be a completely unexpected aspect pattern. With the publication of a result (which I have invented here by way of example), much more extensive research would have to be undertaken, checking hundreds of horoscopes to see if they would confirm the conclusions. Any research would be likely to be regarded as an "accidental" result, not proving our search.

Great was my astonishment, therefore, when upon closer scrutiny of the available charts, an indication came to light which was both unexpected (not expected, not traditional) and appropriate. The conclusion tied up with other research, which was also obtained by means of navamsa conjunctions, which threw a wholly new light on the astrological side of the matter. The conclusion was simple—in the charts of male homosexuals it is not so much Venus that is afflicted as the Moon. And by afflicted we understand a navamsa conjunction with Saturn or a strong influence from houses six or twelve. In other words, the same horoscope points which (in the two cases studied in the previous chapter) seemed so fatal when they affected the Sun, Moon, and the third house, have a part to play here too: they disturb an important function—that of the Moon.

Before going into the consequences of this for theorizing about homosexuality, we shall make our position clearer by means of representative examples. Chart 3 presents a clear example of the discovered pattern in its most emphatic form. At first sight, the horoscope offers little information: the position of Uranus in the fifth house (romance) is interesting; note also the conjunction of Sun and Pluto close to the MC. Given a little imagination, both indications could be called appropriate: the traditional planet of homosexuality is in the house of love and eroticism, and Pluto (ruler of Scorpio), *the* planet of sexual drive, is prominently placed in the zodiac through its conjunction with the Sun. Pluto is also prominent in the houses because of its conjunction with the MC. But this is not a pattern that we regularly find in charts of known homosexuals.

Another striking position is that of the Moon and the Ascendant. This Moon, apart from anything else, forms some very strongly pronounced aspects: it is square to the Sun/Pluto conjunction, and it forms a sextile with a conjunction of Saturn and Neptune. There is a fine trine made by Jupiter from the cusp

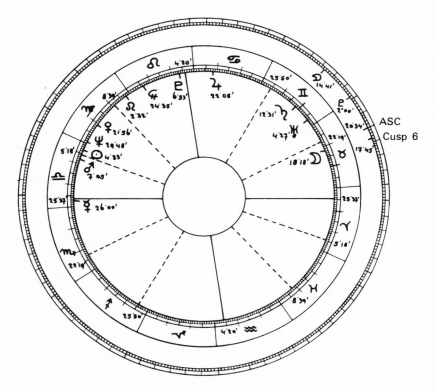

Chart 4. Male Horoscope Number 2. N. lat. 52°01', ST 8h26m41s.

of the ninth house, the best position for this planet. Some astrologers would contest the validity of an aspect like this because it crosses the borders of a sign (the aspect is full in 29° 28' Virgo, not in Libra), but I do not attach so much importance to these boundaries. The position of the Moon is strong and its influence is mixed: the square of the Sun and Pluto (from Cancer—the sign of the Moon) is in itself unfavorable, but against this we have to weigh a sextile from Saturn and Neptune, and the trine from Jupiter. The Moon is lady of the tenth house (social affairs, career), and naturally stands for the masses, the public. Thus it will come as no surprise when we reveal that this is the chart of the late Wim Sonneveld, a well-known cabaret performer on the continent.

So what are the signs of homosexuality in this horoscope? The navamsa position of Saturn is 3° 07′ Aries, conjunct with navamsa cusp twelve. Both are conjunct the Descendant, the point of fixed relationships and of the marriage partner. Chiron stands here also, signifying that at this place a connection is expressed between the Moon, Saturn, the twelfth house, and love relationships. For those who follow Carter (see Chapter 2) by looking at the three outer planets for homosexual inclinations, it will be interesting to observe that navamsa Uranus and navamsa Neptune both stand in the first degrees of Taurus and are therefore practically conjunct the cusp of the eighth house. What is more, navamsa Pluto is conjunct radical Neptune, so that these three planets are all interconnected.

The next horoscope example is Chart 4 (Male Number 2). Just as in Chart 3, Pluto is close to the MC, this time not in conjunction with the Sun but in sextile to it. Uranus stands not in the fifth but in the eighth house, another house which has to do with sexuality (in my opinion, the fifth house represents sexual pleasures and the eighth house the sexual urge). Hence there is a certain degree of similarity to Chart 3, but the similarity is not great at first glance—that is, until we study the navamsa positions—then we find that navamsa Moon conjuncts Saturn and navamsa cusp six conjuncts the Moon. Using traditional methods, we should, in addition to the placement of Pluto, notice the positions of the typically masculine planets—the Sun and Mars—in the twelfth house. And our conclusion would be that these planets, both debilitated in Libra (where the Sun is in its fall, and Mars in its detriment), are pointers here to an "enervated manhood."

The third male example is Chart 5 on page 44. Here the connection between Saturn and the Moon is very strong indeed: the Moon is in Capricorn and is therefore ruled by Saturn, but also navamsa Saturn conjuncts the Moon. Radical Saturn is in the twelfth house and cusp twelve plays a debilitating role: its

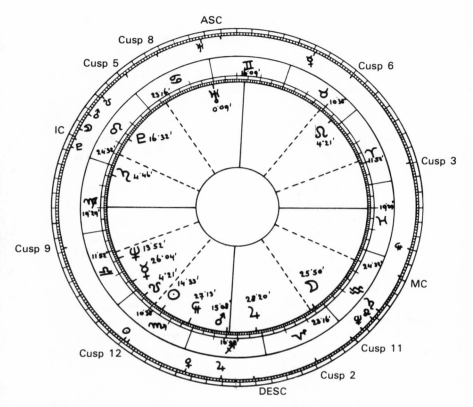

Chart 5. Male Horoscope Number 3. N. lat. 52°22′, ST 4h35m08s.

navamsa position is not on the Moon but on the Venus/Mars conjunction in the seventh house in Virgo. Since Venus and Mars represent the partners in an erotic relationship, and are posited in the house of relationships, this is an appropriate indication to consider. The unfortunate position of the Moon is further strengthened by a conjunction with the navamsa MC.

In Chart 6 the pattern emerges again quite clearly. The navamsa Moon is almost in conjunction with radical cusp twelve and a few degrees below this cusp we find Saturn. In addition, the Moon is the ruler of the twelfth house. Chart 7, on page 46,

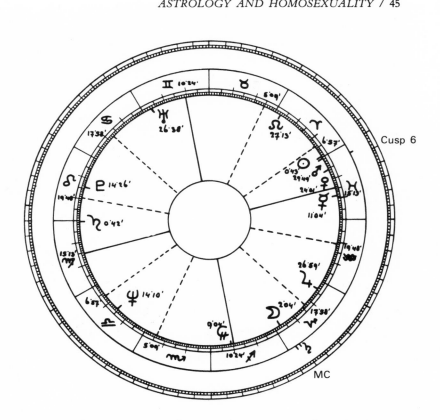

Chart 6. Male Horoscope Number 4. N. lat. 52°14', ST 2h21m10s.

has a navamsa Moon conjunct radical cusp six, and navamsa cusp twelve conjunct the Moon. Radical Saturn plays a somewhat less pronounced role than in Charts 3-6. It is trine the Moon.

In Chart 8 the Moon rules the twelfth house, stands in the twelfth house and is conjunct navamsa cusp twelve! (See page 47.) Saturn squares the Moon from its own tenth house. These two horoscopes are clearly of the same type. That in Chart 7 the connection between Saturn and the Moon is a trine need not surprise us, since the two planets are incompatible and rule opposing signs (Cancer and Capricorn), and Saturn is a malefic

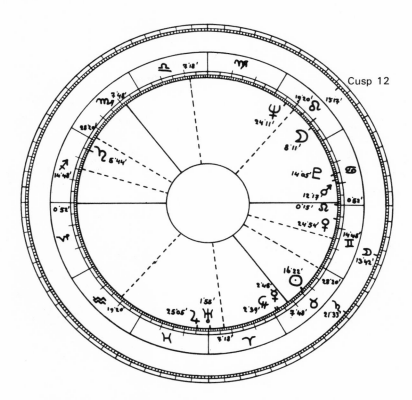

Chart 7. Male Horoscope Number 5. N. lat. 52°33′, ST 14h21m45s.

which is placed higher than the Moon in this particular horoscope. Note, too, that Saturn is lord of the Ascendant and therefore carries extra weight.

Chart 9, on page 48, has navamsa Moon conjunct navamsa Saturn, and radical Saturn stands with Venus just below cusp twelve. Radical Pluto, ruler of the twelfth house, stands a few degrees from the navamsa conjunction of Moon and Saturn, while navamsa Pluto has a prominent position in its own sign on the Ascendant. As we might imagine, the native is a passionate man (Pluto strong on the Ascendant), but leads a solitary love

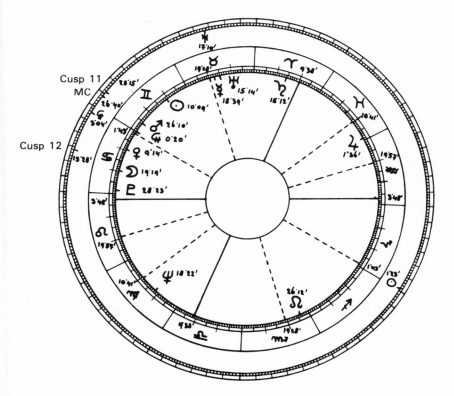

Chart 8. Male Horoscope Number 6. N. lat. 52°36′, ST 0h35m23s.

life. Venus, the classical ruler of the seventh house (now replaced in this rulership by Chiron, but still influential in the house to some extent) is in this instance the literal ruler of seven (since Taurus is on the cusp), and is posited in the twelfth house in its detriment, conjunct with Saturn. A more unfortunate position can hardly be conceived.

The pattern we are here discussing (Moon, Saturn and the houses of hardship—six and twelve—in interaction) need not always show itself in navamsa conjunctions. As we have already seen, this pattern can also be found when traditional methods are

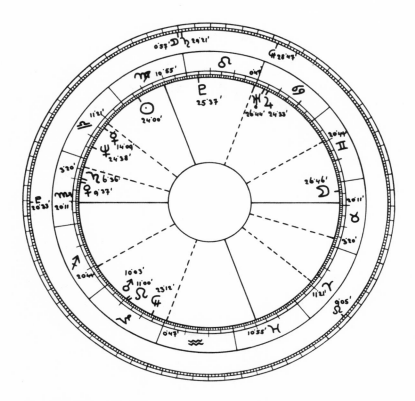

Chart 9. Male Horoscope Number 7. N. lat. 52°26′, ST 10h49m35s.

employed, though much less frequently. A good example of this is Chart 10. Here we see Saturn in Cancer (the sign of the Moon) plumb on the Ascendant, with the Moon making a square with Saturn and the Ascendant from the fifth house (eroticism). The ruler of the twelfth house (Venus) makes a navamsa conjunction with the Moon. The natural lord of the twelfth (Neptune) is conjunct the Moon in the ordinary way and therefore with cusp five as well. It is amazing how the same pattern is repeated here by other means.

Compare Chart 11 with this—see page 50. Here radical Moon and radical Saturn are in close conjunction in the fifth

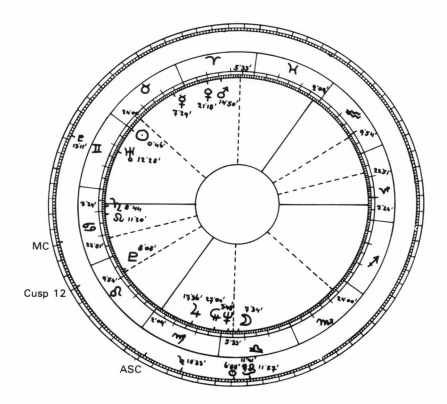

Chart 10. Male Horoscope Number 8. N. lat. 52°25′, ST 22h16m33s.

house. Navamsa cusp six is in wide conjunction with these two planets. If we assume that the actual time of birth was two minutes earlier than given, the conjunction is exact. If you feel that to make such an assumption would be going to far, we still obtain a reasonable conjunction with the navamsa MC for the stated time given for the birth.

Finally, take a look at Chart 12 on page 51. At first sight we see nothing more than a fairly wide navamsa conjunction between cusp twelve and the radical Moon. Certainly the navamsa Moon does not make a conjunction with radical Saturn. The orb amounts to almost thirty degrees, which is far too great, especially when

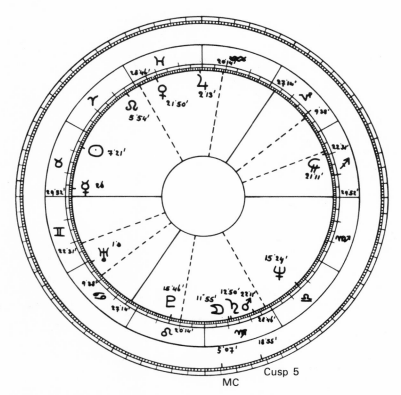

Chart 11. Male Horoscope Number 9. N. lat. 52°22', ST 19h57m11s.

allowances are made for a possible error in the birth time. However, we do see the Sun (lord of the twelfth house) in navamsa conjunction with the Moon within a very narrow orb. Very interesting, too, is the position of navamsa Saturn conjunct the IC. The Moon is the natural lady of this house, so the native's lunar function appears to be afflicted by Saturn.

A special case is shown in Chart 13 on page 52. This is the horoscope of Gerard Reve, the Dutch "people's writer" as he likes to call himself. Over the years he has made himself fairly notorious, on the one hand, by his avowedly homosexual

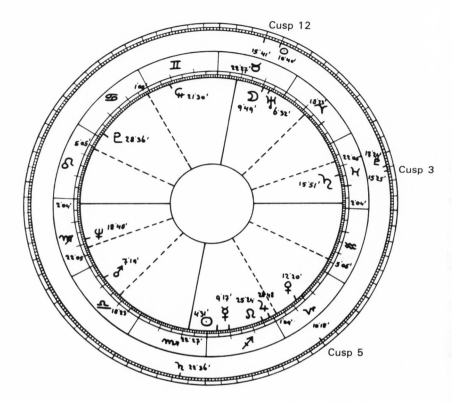

Chart 12. Male Horoscope Number 10. N. lat. 51°55′, ST 3h20m12.

literature interlarded with sadomasochistic elements; on the other hand, by his veneration of the Queen of the Netherlands, and, in recent years, the Virgin Mary. It is extremely likely that he is transferring his feelings for his dead mother to these archetypal mother-figures.

The mother, the sovereign lady, the goddess, the motherland, are all concepts which come under rulership of the Moon. It is immediately obvious that the Moon in Chart 13 is very powerful: conjunct the MC and Uranus, trining Pluto in the twelfth house, and sextile Venus. Anyone with a strong Moon

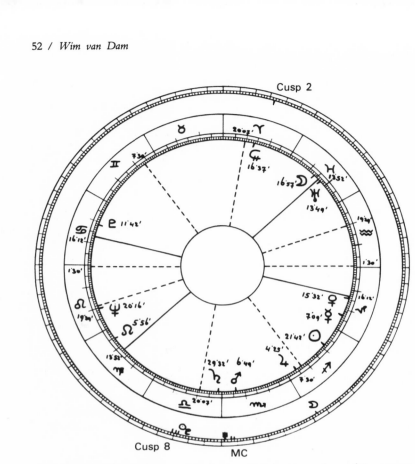

Chart 13. Gerard Reve. Born December 14, 1923 in Amsterdam. N. lat. 52°22′, E. long. 4°55′, GT 17.11.30. ST 23h00m34s.

like this would know how to attract the attention of the public at large by some kind of bizarre (Uranus) behavior. Just as in the horoscope of Wim Sonneveld, the connection between the Moon and the public is very plain. That Reve is an inspired writer appears from the position of Neptune (inspiration) right on the cusp of the third house (authorship), in Leo (creativity) and in trine with the lord of Leo, the Sun, in the sixth (occupation). The success Reve reaped for so many years is intimated by the position of the very favorable fixed star Achernar (Pisces 14° 10′) on the MC (social status).

The sadomasochistic traits in his character may be symbolized by the Venus/Pluto opposition from the sixth to the twelfth house, or by the position of navamsa Mars and navamsa MC conjunct Mars in Scorpio in the fifth house, or by navamsa Sun, navamsa Pluto, and navamsa cusp eight conjunct in the fourth house. The fourth house represents the home (the fixed abode) and the energy indicated by the Sun/Pluto conjunction finds an outlet in the continual construction work, toil, and moil in the house of which Reve's books are so full. That his finances are in good shape is due to the navamsa conjunction of cusp two (money) with the beneficial Chiron in the tenth house. The leading parts in Chart 13 are played by the Moon, Uranus and the violent planets Mars, Pluto, and Uranus. The influence of houses six and twelve is obvious, but Saturn preserves a low profile. Possibly Reve was not a homosexual in his youth—he was married to the poetess Hannie Michaelis—and to judge from his books he is still not completely unmoved by female beauty. All in all, he has an unusually fascinating horoscope, full of ups and downs.

But why is the correlation so interesting? Well, in astrology the Sun and Moon serve as archetypal representatives of the male and the female. Mercury has to be seen as definitely bisexual (Hermes + Aphrodite = the Hermaphrodite). The other planets are preponderantly male or female—but never exclusively one of the two—a fact we might have guessed from the double rulerships of the classical planets, each of which ruled two signs (a male or odd sign, and a female or even sign). The Sun and Moon, however, rule one sign each: the Sun rules masculine Leo and the Moon rules feminine Cancer. Hence they are the outstanding representatives of male and female in astrology.

If it is really the case, as argued above, that the Moon is with surprising frequency weak (afflicted) in the charts of male homosexuals, this leads to an unexpected but not altogether impossible conclusion: what distinguishes homosexual men from heterosexual men is not, as is so often supposed, a lack of manhood (which might show up in an afflicted Sun) but, strange to say, a lack of femininity. We are inevitably reminded of the theory of animus and anima in Jungian psychology, which postulates that every man normally has an unconscious feminine part in his character (the anima) and every woman has a corresponding male half (the animus). Guided by nature or social pressures, each man suppresses his feminine character traits, but unconsciously keeps searching for the woman who will represent these unconscious character traits for him. Such a woman will arouse his feelings of love. Of course, the same is true for a woman, who instinctively unveils, in the man of her choice, her own unconscious male character traits. Therefore it seems reasonable to conclude that homosexuals have a shortage of feminine components in their characters, and therefore could be considered somewhat incomplete. This hypothesis throws a new light on the demonstrative behavior of some homosexuals, which may be an overcompensation for a deficiency rather than the working off of a surplus of femininity, as is often surmised.

The theory just proposed does suffer one disadvantage—it is partly unprovable. An important role is invariably played by house cusps and, above all, by navamsa positions. If there is any error in the stated time of birth, navamsa positions can be thrown considerably out of true—an average nine degrees for every mistake of four minutes in time. Therefore only accurately registered times can be used, and these are difficult to obtain. The mutual navamsa conjunctions between Moon and Saturn are much less sensitive to variations in time, but with the Moon we need to consider the fact that calculations made from positions given in the ephemerides can be out by as much as one degree. This is not due to changes in the Moon's rate of motion (which causes no more than a few minutes of arc variation) but due to the phenomenon of parallax. The latter is an apparent displacement in the Moon's position caused by the relative nearness of the Moon to the Earth. As seen from the place of observation (that is to say, from the birth place), the Moon is seldom or never where it ought to be by simple reckoning. In the light of experience, I have come to believe that allowance must always be made for this displacement when a horoscope is being cast. All the charts given in this book show the Moon's place corrected for parallax.

It would be incorrect to pretend that the pattern of "Moon-and-Saturn-plus-houses-six-and-twelve" is invariably found in the horoscopes of homosexuals. The majority (three quarters) of the cases studied display this pattern more or less clearly; some cases make the interpretation look rather forced and a few cases seem to be exceptions to the rule. There is no need to resort to the explanation that the stated time of birth is wrong in these exceptions, although doubtless that is sometimes the case. It is more sensible to accept that not all forms of homosexuality contains the same elements, and that extensive research might well bring other patterns to light. However, in the majority of cases, the rule we have just discovered appears to be a sufficient explanation.

CONSISTENCY WITH EXISTING THEORIES

According to some psychologists, where there is no innate predisposition, the influence of the mother is important for the development of homosexuality. By dominating her son and capturing his emotions so that they continually flow out to her, she makes it impossible for him to love any other woman in the normal way. Her son might feel that any warmth directed to another woman either consciously or unconsciously would be an act of betrayal towards his so affectionate mother-figure.

To my own way of thinking, this is a rather primitive theory, but it cannot be denied that this type of homosexual does exist. We all know of homosexuals who live at home with mother to the end, never dreaming of taking a vacation alone, seeming to adore her beyond all reason. Since the mother-figure is represented by the Moon, and since the Moon seems to be so clearly affected in homosexuality, our investigations do appear to lend support to the theory. But this would mean that a *weakened* Moon indicates a *dominant* mother. However, in astrology we often see that a weak point in the horoscope can be very significant because it gives rise to overcompensation. From this point of view we could say that the homosexuals in question compensate for a lack of feminine character traits by excessive identification with their mothers.

6. COMPARISON WITH HEIMSOTH'S EXAMPLES

It is a well-known phenomenon in astrological (and other!) types of research that initially very clear and consistent results are obtained which fail to reappear at a later stage, especially when more cases have been studied. The investigation described in the previous chapter relates to a small sample of some 40 cases and therefore our findings cannot be regarded as definite. However, they should prove to be a stimulus to the astrological world, both to take a closer look at the subject of homosexuality, and to use the technique of navamsa conjunctions when examining other groups. The present results need checking by repeating the study on a larger scale, with the help of accurately recorded birth times.

To begin with, let's look at some of the example cases presented by Heimsoth.[12] Chart 14 on page 58 is the horoscope of Haarmann. This formerly notorious sex-crazed killer brutally murdered dozens of young boys, whose remains he then boned and concealed. His trial created quite a stir at the beginning of

---

[12]Some of the more interesting horoscopes that were used as examples in Heimsoth, *Homosexuality in the Horoscope*, are presented here for the Dutch reader. English readers should note that this book was translated into English by Richard S. Baldwin, and published by the American Federation of Astrologers, Tempe, Arizona, in 1978. Further study of the case histories we mention in this book may be of interest to the serious researcher, and the English version of the book should still be available from the AFA.

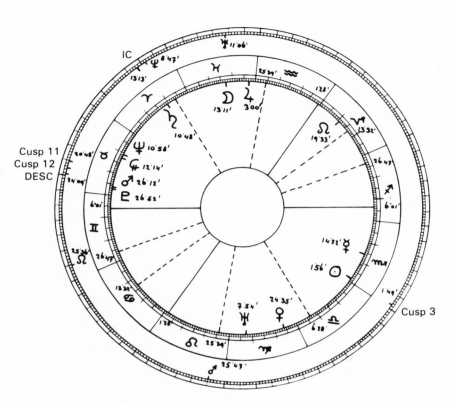

Chart 14. Haarmann. Born October 25, 1879 in Hanover. N. lat. 52°22′, E. long. 9°44′, GT 17.21, ST 20h15m40s. (See also Heimsoth's discussion in *Homosexuality in the Horoscope*, American Federation of Astrologers, Tempe, Ariz., 1978.)

the 1920's. Haarmann regarded himself as being incurably insane, and declared that he would not be able to prevent himself from committing the same crimes all over again if he had the chance. He pleaded—not for imprisonment or hard labor—but for the death sentence, claiming that death meant no more to him than an operation that was over in a few moments. His wish was granted and he was executed on April 15, 1925.

His was a gruesome and bizarre life. Can we regard him as a normal homosexual? Some homosexuals have a love-hate

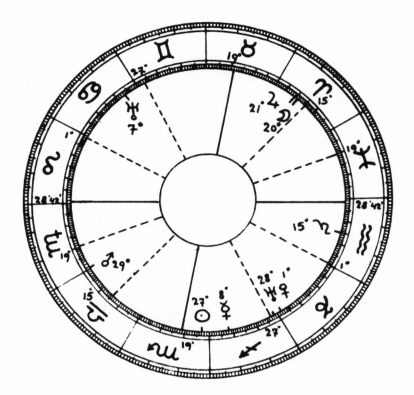

Chart 15. Figure 6 from Heimsoth's *Homosexuality in the Horoscope.* The actual case study has been translated into English and published (in 1978) by the American Federation of Astrologers, Tempe, Arizona.

relationship with their sexual partners. In this horoscope we can see our familiar indications in respect to the Moon, Saturn, and the twelfth house, but they manifest in a different manner. Saturn is in its fall, a few degrees below the cusp of the twelfth house. The Moon is not afflicted by Saturn or by the twelfth house, but is conjunct navamsa Uranus, the lord of the tenth house. The most striking indication of homicidal tendencies is the conjunction between Mars and Pluto in the twelfth house under the rays of the fixed star Algol (Taurus 25° 3'). In Greek

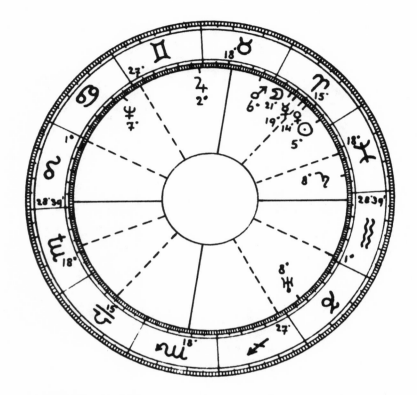

Chart 16. Figure 8 from Heimsoth's *Homosexuality in the Horoscope*. The actual case study has been translated into English and published (in 1978) by the American Federation of Astrologers, Tempe, Arizona.

mythology, this star is associated with Medusa, whose ghastly stare turned to stone whoever looked at her. Algol is reputed to be the most dangerous and murderous of all the fixed stars—a reputation that was reinforced by the fact that Mars was in conjunction with it when the first atomic bomb exploded. Algol is a variable star and its influence is most baneful when its light is dimmest. The story goes that, in the Middle Ages, Arab generals would never launch an attack when Algol's light was faint. Therefore it need hardly surprise us to see the two planets of

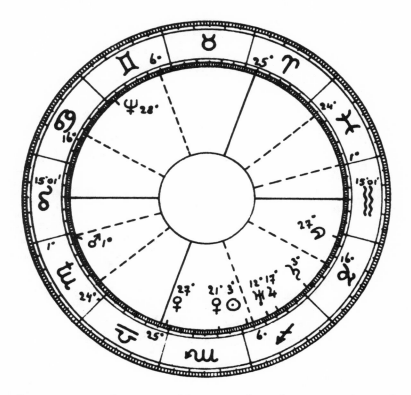

Chart 17. Figure 11 from Heimsoth's *Homosexuality in the Horoscope*. The actual case study has been translated into English and published (in 1978) by the American Federation of Astrologers, Tempe, Arizona.

murder and aggression (both rulers of Scorpio) joining forces with this particular star. The twelfth house placement is appropriate both to the secret character of the deeds and to possible homosexual tendencies. Personally, I do not attach too much importance to this, for the conjunction makes no aspect with a cusp in the chart. It is all the more striking, therefore, that the navamsa Ascendant/Descendant axis falls över the placement *and* so does navamsa cusp twelve. Once more we find navamsa conjunctions emphasizing something which, though obviously

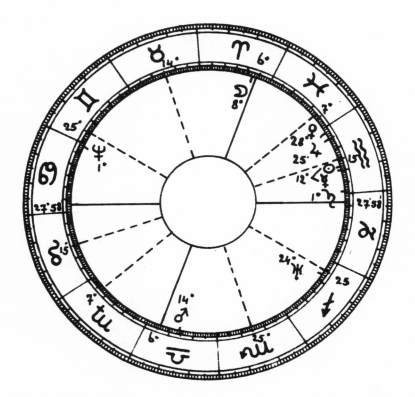

Chart 18. Figure 12 from Heimsoth's *Homosexuality in the Horoscope*. The actual case study has been translated into English and published (in 1978) by the American Federation of Astrologers, Tempe, Arizona.

applicable, is not really prominent. Saturn's position in the twelfth house is emphasized because the navamsa IC is in conjunction with it. Note, too, that the position of navamsa Mars is exactly on cusp five.

As already mentioned, Saturn is posited as might have been expected in Chart 14, but the position of the Moon is rather aberrant, for she stands in navamsa conjunction with the inherently favorable fixed star Achernar (Pisces 14° 10′) which bestows fame and honor. In a negative sense Achernar's promise was brilliantly fulfilled: the trial aroused tremendous interest,

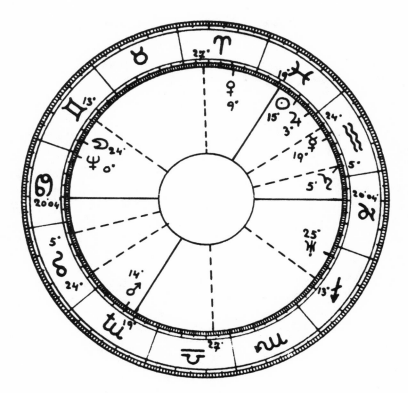

Chart 19. This is Heimsoth's Case 13. From *Homosexuality in the Horoscope*. The actual case study was published in 1978 in English by the American Federation of Astrologers, Tempe, Arizona.

receiving the publicity that might have been expected with the Moon as lady of the third house (the press). There is a marked similarity here to Gerard Reve's horoscope (see Chart 13 on page 52), which has an ordinary conjunction of the Moon and Uranus with Achernar. Fortunately Reve's Mars is in trine, not in conjunction, with Pluto, and his Moon is nicely aspected too. The shared adverse features may have something to do with the sadomaschism in the characters of the two natives.

If we use example charts found in Heimsoth's study, we must remember that he rounded off the positions of the cusps and

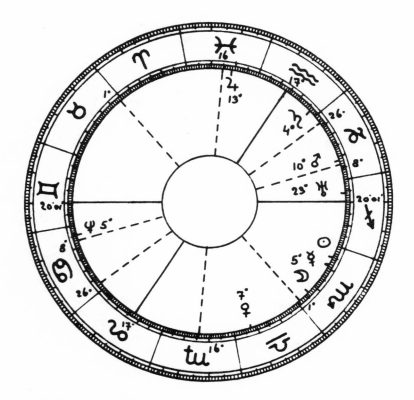

Chart 20. This is Heimsoth's Case 14. From *Homosexuality in the Horoscope*. The actual case study was published in 1978 in English by the American Federation of Astrologers, Tempe, Arizona.

planets to the nearest degree. With a one degree orb, the typical pattern may appear to emerge without really being present. In other words, it could be an artifact. As an example, Heimsoth's figure 6, Chart 15 on page 59, has navamsa cusp twelve seemingly in conjunction with the Moon; Saturn being in the sixth in navamsa conjunction with itself and thus very strongly placed. Chart 16 on page 60 (Heimsoth's figure 8), shows navamsa cusp twelve apparently in conjunction with the Moon. Chart 17 on page 61 (Heimsoth's figure 11) is very interesting as well: the Moon is lady of the twelfth and stands in detriment in

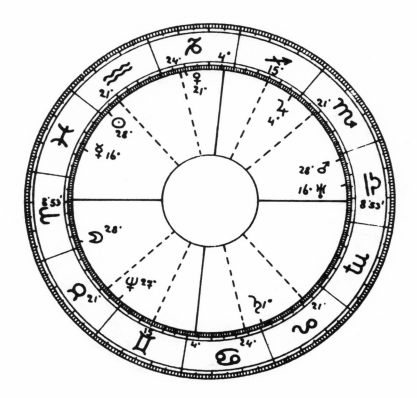

Chart 21. Case 15 from Heimsoth, *Homosexuality in the Horoscope*. The actual case study was published in 1978 in English by the American Federation of Astrologers, Tempe, Arizona.

the sixth. With her is navamsa Saturn, lord of the sixth house. This is, therefore, a case where our rule very clearly applies, and it occasions great satisfaction that it is one of the few instances in which the author (Heimsoth) unequivocally declares that the native was a homosexual by choice.

Heimsoth's horoscope 12 (our Chart 18 on page 62), is not so clear-cut. After the native's mother died, he began to suffer from hallucinations regarding his lady friend, in which, for example, he saw her nose increasing in size. Whether this was a homosexual fantasy is not entirely clear, but that the trouble had

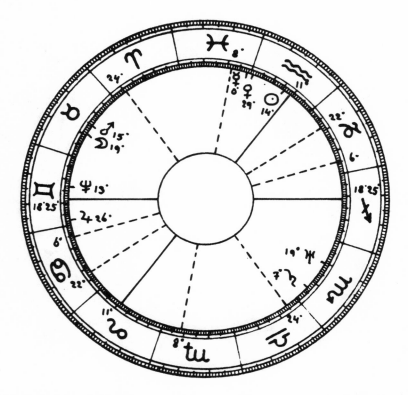

Chart 22. Heimsoth's Case 16. From *Homosexuality in the Horoscope*. The actual case study was published in 1978 in English by the American Federation of Astrologers, Tempe, Arizona.

something to do with his mother could follow from the conjunction of navamsa Saturn with the IC from where it opposes the radical Moon. (Bear in mind that although navamsa positions work only by means of conjunctions, they also share in the aspects of the radical points with which they are conjunct.) There is a likely navamsa conjunction of the Moon with cusp twelve. Heimsoth says of his case 13 (Chart 19 on page 63) the native was hard to pin down with regard to his sexual preferences, "but could safely be considered effeminate and homosexual." The only possible indication according to our own

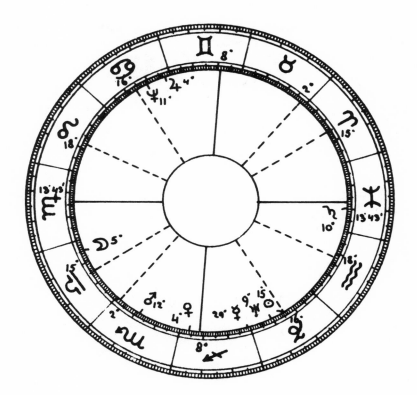

Chart 23. Heimsoth's Case 18. From *Homosexuality in the Horoscope*. The actual case study was published in 1978 in English by the American Federation of Astrologers, Tempe, Arizona.

theory would be the position of the Moon in the twelfth house. In Case 14 (Chart 20 on page 64), just as in Case 11 (Chart 17) the Moon is in the sixth house, conjunct with navamsa Saturn. Chart 21 (on page 65) shows navamsa Saturn conjunct with navamsa cusp twelve, both right on the Ascendant. The lord of the twelfth house, Uranus, is in navamsa conjunction with cusp twelve, and the Moon in the first house is square to Saturn. Chart 22 is a reproduction of Heimsoth's figure 16. Saturn is in the sixth; the ruler of the twelfth is in the twelfth house, where we also find its navamsa position. It is conjunct the Moon as well. The navamsa

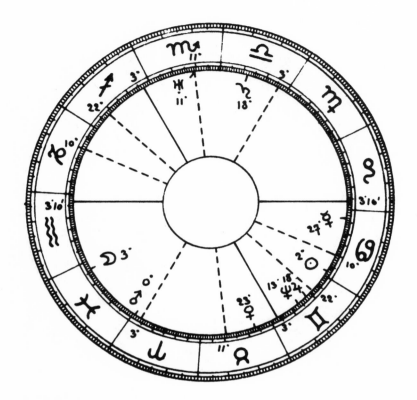

Chart 24. Heimsoth's Case 20. From *Homosexuality in the Horoscope*. The actual case study was published in 1978 in English by the American Federation of Astrologers, Tempe, Arizona.

Moon is 21 Gemini, conjunct the Ascendant, which emphasizes the significance of the twelfth house position of this planet.

Heimsoth states that there was absolutely no doubt about homosexuality for Chart 23 on page 67. And what do we find? In his figure 18, navamsa Saturn in conjunction with the Moon, and navamsa cusp six in conjunction with Saturn. Heimsoth's example 20 (Chart 24) is the horoscope of Britain's King Edward VIII, who later became the Duke of Windsor. With the best intentions in the world, we can find not a single indication of homosexuality here. This might be expected, for a king who

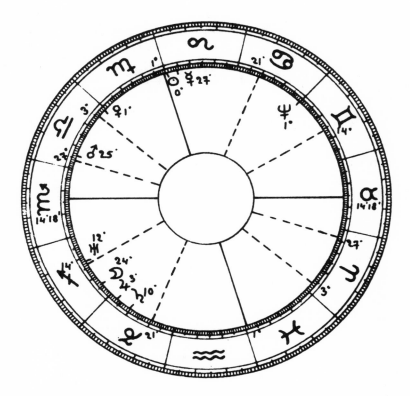

Chart 25. This is Figure 24 in Heimsoth, *Homosexuality in the Horoscope*. For more information about the actual case study, see the English translation published in 1978 by the American Federation of Astrologers, Tempe, Arizona.

abdicates his throne for the love of a woman can hardly be considered homosexual! According to Heimsoth's text, rumors had circulated regarding the Duke's sexual tastes when he was Prince of Wales, but, as we saw in Chapter 2, Heimsoth took pleasure in branding practically all the members of royal houses down the centuries as either covert or obvious homosexuals without much hard evidence for most of his allegations.

Most of Heimsoth's cases are described as sexually inhibited or neurotic. Only in Chart 25 (Heimsoth's figure 24) is it asserted that the person concerned was a known male homosexual. The sole indications of this are wide conjunctions between cusp six and the Moon and the Moon with cusp twelve. Given the required orb for our study, this is obviously not good enough.

We conclude that, allowing for the imprecision of Heimsoth's material, the results seem to fall in line with those of our own investigation. We note a clear trend involving the interaction of the Moon, Saturn, and houses six and twelve when attempting to determine the factor of male homosexuality in the birth chart.

7. FEMALE HOMOSEXUALITY

Very little has been written about female homosexuality from an astrological point of view. Heimsoth devotes a very short chapter to the subject without presenting a single example chart. He states that female homosexuality, unlike the male variety, falls not under Uranus but under Neptune. His conclusion is that, if the disposition is not inherited, it originates in a neurosis with regard to the mother. Otherwise he has little more to tell us.

After the surprising result announced in Chapter 5, it was natural to expect that the charts of female homosexuals would have the Sun, the representative of the masculine principle, afflicted and not the Moon. In the charts of male homosexuals, female characteristics are under pressure, so we could presume that the male characteristics might be weakened in charts of female homosexuals. However, this hardly seems to be borne out in practice. It is true that some horoscopes investigated show the Sun weakened by Saturn or by cusp twelve, but this could not be turned into a hard-and-fast rule.

Nevertheless, it would appear that the Sun, the male component, is indeed repressed in the horoscopes of lesbians; however, not through its own placement but rather because of domination by some other planet. Although the pattern was not as distinct as the afflicted Moon for males, the planet Uranus

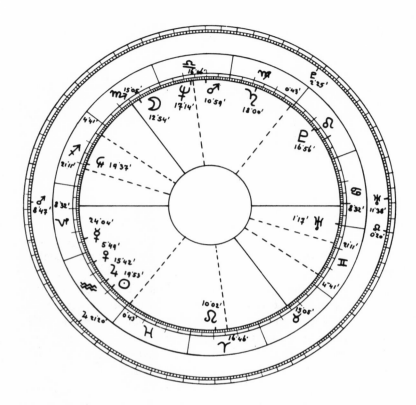

Chart 26. Female Horoscope Number 1. N. lat. 52°05′, ST 14h50m27s.

turned out to be the disturbing factor in just over half the female cases studied. This is in direct conflict with Heimsoth's results.

In my opinion, which I offer with the necessary caution, there is some significance in the fact that Uranus is prominent, usually through a conjunction (navamsa or natal) with the Ascendant/Descendant, and sometimes in some other way. Many cases can be explained by this formula. In cases where Uranus does not apply, I have so far failed to discover any other explanation. It is noteworthy that the very planet that has always been considered an indicator of male homosexuality is implicated in the female cases. Perhaps a few representative examples will

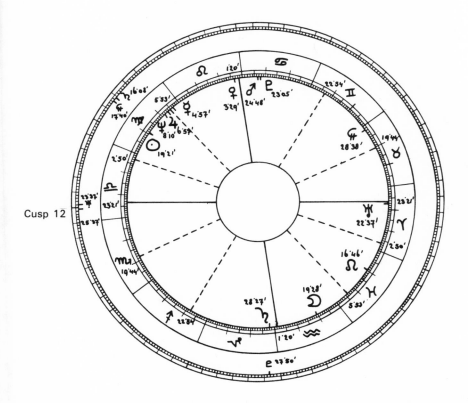

Cusp 12

Chart 27. Female Horoscope Number 2. N. lat. 52°22', ST 8h14m16s.

make this clear. Chart 26 (Female 1) shows Uranus in wide conjunction with the Descendant, while navamsa Uranus is in close conjunction with the same Descendant. In addition, the navamsa Dragon's Head (North Node) is conjunct radical Uranus, and the Dragon's Head is a point which has to do with relationships, just like the Ascendant/Descendant axis.

In Chart 27 (Female 2) we see that radical Uranus is conjunct the radix Descendant; navamsa Uranus is exactly on the Ascendant; navamsa Saturn conjuncts the Sun. Chart 28 on page 74 shows the navamsa Ascendant conjunct radical Uranus. The navamsa Moon conjuncts navamsa Descendant and is therefore

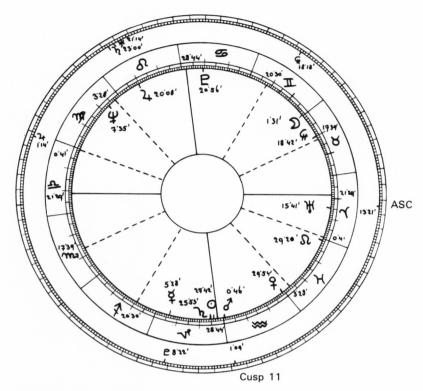

ASC

Cusp 11

Chart 28.* Female Horoscope Number 3. N. lat. 52°22′, ST 8h03m28s.

"connected up" (by transfer of light[13]) with radical Uranus. Chart 29 shows us an ordinary Uranus/Descendant conjunction. The fact that it is in its own sign intensifies the action of Uranus. In Chart 30 page 76 the Ascendant conjuncts navamsa Uranus. Thus we see a pattern of Uranus in (navamsa) conjunction with the Ascendant or Descendant which keeps recurring in the charts

---

[13]But see earlier note on traditional meaning of "translation of light." *Tr.*

*Our editor questioned this chart. Although birth data was unavailable, it seems as though houses were calculated for one day and planets another. Serious researchers should note this. *Pub.*

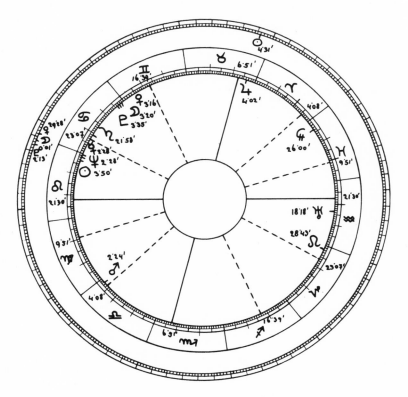

Chart 29. Female Horoscope Number 4. N. lat. 52°22′, ST 2h18m01s.

of lesbians, even though it does so less often than does the Moon-
Saturn-twelfth-cusp pattern seen in charts of male homosexuals.
An example of a different kind is Chart 31 (page 77) in which
there is no direct contact between Uranus and the cusps, but
where Uranus does stand in the first house, conjunct the navamsa
Moon, navamsa Dragon's Head and navamsa Neptune. Neptune
is lord of the first house, so that Uranus in the first, conjunct the
navamsa Neptune, symbolizes, virtually, an afflicted Ascendant.
Although this pattern (a dominant Uranus in the Ascendant/
Descendant axis of personal relationships) does not always show
up, we encounter it with impressive frequency and certainly

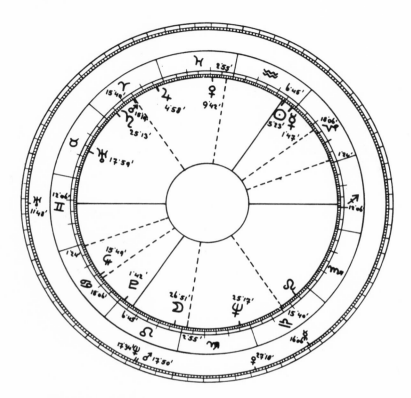

Chart 30. Female Horoscope Number 5. N. lat. 51°55′, ST 20h36m34s.

more often than the afflicted Sun we originally expected. What are the consequences for this theory?

Uranus is the natural enemy of the Sun. These two planets rule opposing signs (Aquarius and Leo respectively) and therefore have little "affection" for one another. Uranus is a rebel and likes to take an independent line; there will always be something strange about those born under this influence. The Sun, on the other hand, is a stable, constant force, utterly different from the unpredictable Uranus. When the dominant position of Uranus is chiefly brought to bear on the Ascendant/Descendant axis, this can imply that the Sun (the male component in the psyche)—

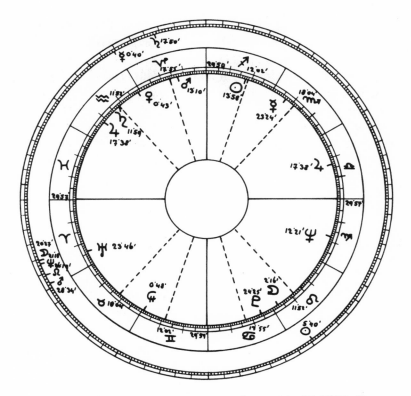

Chart 31. Female Horoscope Number 6. N. lat. 52°05′, ST 17h59m55s.

although it need not be any weaker in lesbians than in heterosexual women—is pushed into the background by the freakish and capricious Uranus, which likes to fly in the face of convention. It experiences the Sun as opposing its own influence. Uranus is a predominantly "male" planet; therefore lesbians, far from having a shortage of male traits, may have a surplus of them. These male characteristics may also be expressed in an unusual way, due to the nature of Uranus.

This leads to a very interesting conclusion: on the face of it we would assume that, in principle, sexuality in both men and women runs along much the same lines, *via* the same pathways in the brain. A deficiency of male characteristics in men or female characteristics in women should, from the point of view of conventional wisdom, be responsible for homosexuality. We have seen, however, that the real causes seem to be a shortage of female characteristics in men and a surplus (not a shortage) of masculinity in women. In other words, the basic masculinity and femininity are normal and it is the balancing part of the personality (the animus or anima) that carries more or less weight than usual.[14] This result was quite unexpected, and needs further testing and study.

---

[14]This sentence has been added to bring out a little more clearly what the author is saying. The picture that emerges is that in the male homosexual the sexual drive remains intact but the natural interest in sexual relations with women is blocked or underactive. The pattern found for female homosexuals is, or so our author informs us, common but by no means universal. In view of its nature, one would expect that it is peculiar to the more active type of female homosexual, in whom the more "feminine" characteristics have been swamped by an upsurge of "mannishness." This would still leave the astro-psychology of the passive lesbian to be studied. *Tr.*

8. TRANSSEXUALITY

A phenomenon that is essentially different from homo-sexuality is so-called transsexuality. The homosexual has a preference for or is emotionally aroused by persons of the same sex and has incorporated this into his or her lifestyle. The male homosexual does not feel that he is a woman, but a man who is attracted to men. The same is true of lesbians in regard to women. They do not think of themselves as "failed men."[15] In sharp contrast, we have the transsexual. The latter has the feeling from a very early age that he or she is inhabiting a body of the wrong sex. The boy feels he is really a girl, and the girl feels that her ostensible sex is a fault of nature. Certain of these individuals have been treated by surgery or by hormones in recent years. Sex changes are no longer an oddity, even though in the Netherlands stringent tests are required before treatment is permitted, and in France the practice is illegal apart from a few exceptions. More recently the treatment has been extended to help women who want to become men.

---

[15]The author may be missing the implications of his own findings here. He has already pointed out the dominance of the ultra-masculine planet Uranus in the charts of a relatively high proportion of lesbians studied; perhaps some of them really do want to exude a sort of "maleness"? Even before these studies became fashionable, one could always meet the occasional woman who sported mannish clothes and close-cropped hair, yet was by no means ripe for any sex change. Tr.

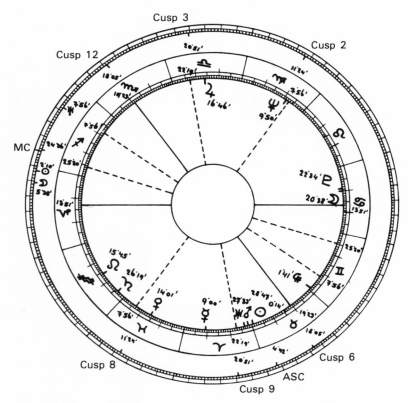

Chart 32. Transsexual Horoscope Number 1. N. lat. 51°35′, ST 15h07m43s.

For the purposes of this study, we have managed to secure the reliable horoscopes of four women who originally came into the world as males but later underwent sex-change operations. Although four horoscopes are not sufficient for statistical analysis, they do display an interesting pattern from which we have drawn some tentative conclusions we should like to share with the reader.

In the first transsexual horoscope, Chart 32, we see a conjunction of navamsa Sun and Moon in the twelfth house. The twelfth house is still further stressed (see Chapter 4): navamsa MC conjunct cusp twelve, and navamsa cusp twelve conjunct the MC. It is plain that the native has experienced great loneliness.

But not in the same manner as the two cases of microcephaly, because the rulers of the third and ninth houses are not affected here.

The reason for a lonely and retiring lifestyle must be sought in the above-mentioned navamsa conjunction of the Sun and Moon in the twelfth house. Here we have a clash of masculinity (the Sun) and femininity (the Moon) in the most unfortunate part of the horoscope, the twelfth house, termed by Ptolemy the house of the evil daimon (evil tutelary spirit). This Sun/Moon conjunction is reinforced by the conjunction of the navamsa Ascendant with the radical Sun. The Moon is afflicted in the seventh house, not by Saturn but by Pluto. However, the Moon is posited in her own sign and is also the lady of the seventh house, so she is more strongly placed than Pluto; therefore femininity (the Moon) comes out on top through transformation (Pluto). Those who regard Uranus as the main cause of sexual "aberrations" will be interested to see that navamsa Uranus is within a minute of arc of cusp eleven.

Chart 33 (see page 82) is the least telling of the four examples. Only the opposition of Mercury—the hermaphrodite—with Uranus, Mercury being right on the horizon, seems to have much significance. However, cusp twelve is prominent: navamsa MC is in conjunction with it. The Moon stands in a position we have seen often enough in the horoscopes of homosexuals: she is in the sixth house square Saturn. At the same time, however, the Moon trines Pluto in Cancer, which is the Moon's own sign. We can make no definite pronouncement on the position of the Sun— not only does it stand in the sign of its fall (rather ominously in the first house), but the navamsa position at 21° 03' Aries is opposing its own radical position within one degree! Whether this means something or not has not yet been settled, but other examples appear to indicate that a self-affliction of this sort weakens the planet concerned. Anyway, we have a Sun/Sun opposition between the radical and the navamsa charts.

In this conjecture we are also supported by Chart 34. Here we see the Sun in Scorpio in the second house, debilitated by a very precise opposition to the Moon. Navamsa Saturn is also conjunct navamsa Moon in the seventh house. The Sun/Moon opposition is

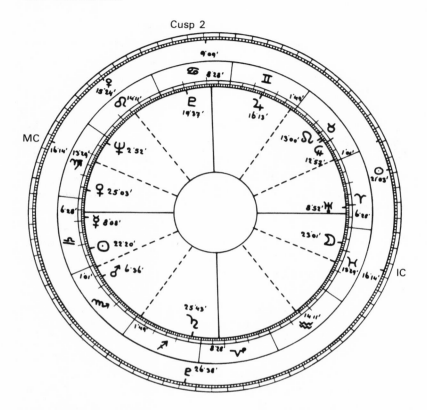

Chart 33. Transsexual Horoscope Number 2. N. lat. 51°55′, ST 6h36m53s.

personalized by the placement of the navamsa Sun conjunct the Ascendant. Navamsa cusp twelve is conjunct not the MC, but Chiron, leading us to the conclusion that in this nativity there is an isolated way of life (twelfth house) due to a disturbed balance (Chiron) that is genetic in character (the fourth house of inheritance). Chart 35 (page 84) has the Sun on the Ascendant, where we also find navamsa cusp six. Once again we see an unfavorable emphasis (the six/twelve axis) on the principle masculine planet, the Sun. The Moon is again in contact with Pluto: by a very close trine from the twelfth house. The Moon is in the fourth house (of inheritance) and Pluto is lord of the fourth.

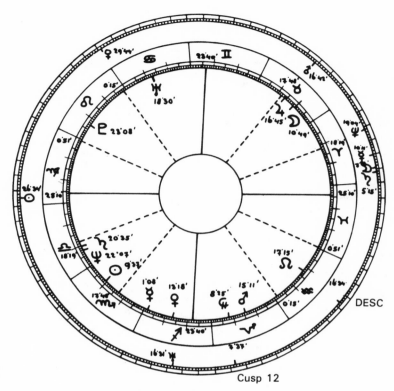

Chart 34. Transsexual Horoscope Number 3. N. lat. 52°04′, ST 5h32m26s.

Although there is no outstanding characteristic common to all four charts, there are several interesting features in various combinations of three of them:

- The Sun is weakly placed in one way or another: Chart 32, 34, 35, (and perhaps in Chart 33 as well);

- A weak Moon: Chart 32, 33, 34, but nowhere seriously so;

- Sun conjunct the Ascendant: Chart 32, 34, 35;

- A strong influence from houses six or twelve: Chart 32, 33, 35;

- Moon in aspect with Pluto: Chart 32, 33, 35.

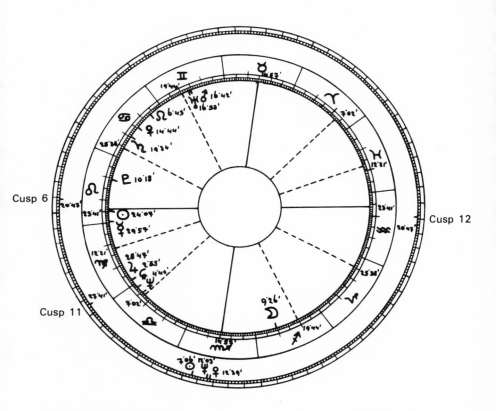

Chart 35. Transsexual Horoscope Number 4. N. lat. 40°38′, ST 5h49m58s.

Each of these features can be considered relevant. The noticeably unfavorable position of the Sun erodes masculinity, the six/twelve axis lays emphasis on isolation or physical defects, and the Moon/Pluto aspect suggests transformation into femininity. Unfortunately the sample is a very small one, and none of the features mentioned can be found in all four charts. It would be interesting to be able to contrast with these some charts of women who have been transformed into men. However, the requisite data has not yet come to hand.

9. SEXUAL IDENTITY

The examples forming the basis of the present study have led us to some interesting conclusions. Whether or not there is any truth in the well-known rule that Uranus is the characteristic planet of the male homosexual, there are no grounds for saying that it becomes so mainly through the conjunction or other aspects with Venus; an assertion currently made in so many words in Mellie Uyldert's *Astrology: the Aspects*, p. 202.[16] Aspects between Uranus and Venus, especially the conjunction and hard aspects, give a love life full of complications, without settled and long-lasting relationships. This is equally true of Venus/Uranus aspects in the charts of heterosexuals. In my opinion it has no particular significance as far as homosexuality is concerned.

The theory that seems to apply in many instances of male homosexuality is that of a Moon afflicted by Saturn or by the unfortunate houses six and twelve. If this is indeed the case, the question arises as to its precise meaning. As always, the materials available to the astrologer are very limited: twelve signs, twelve houses, the Sun, Moon and planets, and the aspects. With this circumscribed vocabulary a whole range of human experience has to be expressed, and each of these elements bears many interpretations.

---

[16]This volume is only available in Dutch as far as we know at the time of this printing. *Pub.*

So, does a Moon afflicted in this fashion represent the mother, the home environment or the genetic make-up? What is the significance of the twelfth and sixth houses respectively: loneliness and separation, a physical defect, a very private lifestyle owing to repression of the emotions? The picture is not altogether clear. And what is the role of Saturn? Does it stand for restriction, so that in male homosexuals we would assume that there is a weakened feminine component of the psyche, or does Saturn stand simply for an inability to relate to women (no interest in them)? These are fundamental questions for astrology. It is just this susceptibility to varied and sometimes conflicting interpretations which has given astrology such a bad name. Its critics say that you can read anything you like into a horoscope after the event.

Consequently our inference must not exceed what can be drawn from the basic meanings of the astrological elements. And this inference is that in the male homosexual the feminine traits (represented by the Moon) are suppressed or weakened. It is impossible to state definitely whether this is due to the influence of the parents (the mother as symbolized by the Moon, the father represented by Saturn), to heredity (the Moon as ruler of the fourth house, Saturn as the shaper of matter), or to traumatic experiences in early life (twelfth house).

The conclusion that surfaced in regard to female homosexuality was quite surprising: Uranus came to the fore as the dominating planet much more clearly than in men; not in aspect with Venus, but through (navamsa) conjunctions with the Ascendant/Descendant axis. However this relationship is less frequent than is the afflicted Moon in the male homosexual, and we know of at least one instance of a woman with a very badly aspected Uranus right on the Ascendant who could certainly not be called lesbian, perhaps because the Sun is also in close and emphatic aspect with the Ascendant. Hence we cannot say simply that female homosexuality is exclusively determined by Uranus in contact with the Ascendant, as the aspect doesn't always indicate that such is the case.

We have been unable to acquire sufficient horoscopes with reliable birth times for transsexual men who have been transformed into women. Our few examples do, however, present an intriguing picture: a weakened Sun, a prominent place for cusps twelve or six, and the Moon in contact with Pluto. This accords well with our *a priori* notions of these people. In connection with the surgical and hormonal treatments, it might be remembered that the Moon stands for the body's fluid economy and rhythms, and Pluto for body chemistry and sexual hormones.

To sum up, we can say that astrological investigation provides no simple explanation covering all male homosexuals, all lesbians and all transsexuals, anyway not in our present state of knowledge. Indeed, it is scarcely to be expected that any such simple explanation will ever be found, unless it turns out that all homosexuals are the same in their homosexuality. That would be very hard to believe; possibly there are as many varieties of homosexuality as there are homosexuals.

Of the conclusions reached, that regarding the women is the least satisfactory, both because the rule applies less often and because it is not so easy to explain. It should be clear by this time, too, that none of our conclusions could have been reached without navamsa conjunctions. Even such a straightforward and obvious phenomenon as the contact between the Moon and Saturn appears very rarely with ordinary aspects. We believe, therefore, that further research into each of the groups studied here will not be able to dispense with the navamsa technique.

APPENDIX:

NAVAMSA TABLES

In order to easily calculate navamsa positions, the following tables have been included here. To look up any navamsa position, you need to use both Tables 1 and 2: Table 1 converts the DEGREES into navamsa degrees (based on whether they are fire, earth, air or water signs) while Table 2 is used to convert minutes in any element into navamsa degrees or minutes. Two examples of how to convert planetary positions into navamsa positions follow:

Example 1. What is the navamsa position of Sun at 2° 58′ Leo?

- Look up 2° longitude under Fire Signs in Table 1. (Note you will find 2° Leo listed correctly only if you use the column marked fire signs.) Your answer will be 18° Aries.

- Then look up 58 minutes in Table 2 in column 3. Your answer is 8°42′.

- Combine the two figures (18° Aries + 8°42′) to locate the navamsa Sun. Your navamsa Sun position would be 26°42′ Aries.

Example 2: To locate the navamsa position for a planet or cusp located at 13°46′ Pisces, you would do the following:

- Go to Table 1 and locate 13° (under WATER signs). Your answer is 27° Libra. 46′ would be located on Table 2 as 6°54′.

- When these two figures are added together (27° Libra + 6°54′) your answer is 33°54′ Libra. As we only have 30° in a sign, this sum needs to be further converted to 3°54′ Scorpio.

Table 1. Converting Degrees into Navamsa Degrees and Signs

Fire Sign		Earth Sign	
Degree	Navamsa Conversion	Degree	Navamsa Conversion
0°	00° ♈	0°	00° ♑
1°	09°	1°	09°
2°	18°	2°	18°
3°	27°	3°	27°
4°	06° ♉	4°	06° ♒
5°	15°	5°	15°
6°	24°	6°	24°
7°	03° ♊	7°	03° ♓
8°	12°	8°	12°
9°	21°	9°	21°
10°	00° ♋	10°	00° ♈
11°	09°	11°	09°
12°	18°	12°	18°
13°	27°	13°	27°
14°	06° ♌	14°	06° ♉
15°	15°	15°	15°
16°	24°	16°	24°
17°	03° ♍	17°	03° ♊
18°	12°	18°	12°
19°	21°	19°	21°
20°	00° ♎	20°	00° ♋
21°	09°	21°	09°
22°	18°	22°	18°
23°	27°	23°	27°
24°	06° ♏	24°	06° ♌
25°	15°	25°	15°
26°	24°	26°	24°
27°	03° ♐	27°	03° ♍
28°	12°	28°	12°
29°	21°	29°	21°

Table 1. Converting Degrees (Continued)

Air Sign		Water Sign	
Degree	Navamsa Conversion	Degree	Navamsa Conversion
0°	00° ♎	0°	00° ♋
1°	09°	1°	09°
2°	18°	2°	18°
3°	27°	3°	27°
4°	06° ♏	4°	06° ♌
5°	15°	5°	15°
6°	24°	6°	24°
7°	03° ♐	7°	03° ♍
8°	12°	8°	12°
9°	21°	9°	21°
10°	00° ♑	10°	00° ♎
11°	09°	11°	09°
12°	18°	12°	18°
13°	27°	13°	27°
14°	06° ♒	14°	06° ♏
15°	15°	15°	15°
16°	24°	16°	24°
17°	03° ♓	17°	03° ♐
18°	12°	18°	12°
19°	21°	19°	21°
20°	00° ♈	20°	00° ♑
21°	09°	21°	09°
22°	18°	22°	18°
23°	27°	23°	27°
24°	06° ♉	24°	06° ♒
25°	15°	25°	15°
26°	24°	26°	24°
27°	03° ♊	27°	03° ♓
28°	12°	28°	12°
29°	21°	29°	21°

Table 2. Converting Minutes into Navamsa Degrees and Minutes

Minutes to Convert	Navamsa Conversion	Minutes to Convert	Navamsa Conversion
0	0° 00′	30	4° 30′
1	0° 09′	31	4° 39′
2	0° 18′	32	4° 48′
3	0° 27′	33	4° 57′
4	0° 36′	34	5° 06′
5	0° 45′	35	5° 15′
6	0° 54′	36	5° 24′
7	1° 03′	37	5° 33′
8	1° 12′	38	5° 42′
9	1° 21′	39	5° 51′
10	1° 30′	40	6° 00′
11	1° 39′	41	6° 09′
12	1° 48′	42	6° 18′
13	1° 57′	43	6° 27′
14	2° 06′	44	6° 36′
15	2° 15′	45	6° 45′
16	2° 24′	46	6° 54′
17	2° 33′	47	7° 03′
18	2° 42′	48	7° 12′
19	2° 51′	49	7° 21′
20	3° 00′	50	7° 30′
21	3° 09′	51	7° 39′
22	3° 18′	52	7° 48′
23	3° 27′	53	7° 57′
24	3° 36′	54	8° 06′
25	3° 45′	55	8° 15′
26	3° 54′	56	8° 24′
27	4° 03′	57	8° 33′
28	4° 12′	58	8° 42′
29	4° 21′	59	8° 51′